Re-framing Your Life
A Guide To Becoming Invincible

By Kimile Pendleton

Re-framing Your Life is a work of nonfiction. Any resemblance to other works or persons, fiction or dead, is purely coincidental.

ISBN-13: 978-1499538953
ISBN-10: 1499538952

Table of Contents

A special thanks to Hank Levin, my mentor and friend, who has supported me personally and professionally for the past 15 years. His expertise in clearing saved me and enabled me to save others. A true genius with people.

A special thanks to all the extraordinary people that I am lucky to call clients. I truly love my work and I am privileged to fulfill my life purpose because of them.

A very special thanks to my family, Tracy my husband, Nathan my son, and Kaitlyn my daughter. Without your love and support this book would not have been possible.

INTRODUCTION

There isn't a person alive whose life goes smoothly. Not the richest person who knows luxury of which the rest of us can only dream, or the poorest monk whose worldly possessions consist of a bed, his shoes, his robe, and the bag of rice that he will cook for dinner. Not the smartest scientist who literally does brain surgery, or the simplest peasant tending his flock.

We may think that others have smooth lives. Certainly, our celebrity-worshipping culture makes us think so. "If only I could walk the red carpet at the Oscars, everything would be fine!" "If only I had ten million dollars in the bank!" "If only my husband would pick up after himself." "If only my wife still looked the way she did when she was twenty."

If only, if only, if only. Our magical thinking is full of "if only." Yet the still, small voice inside us all whispers a fundamental truth: Life isn't smooth, and it isn't easy. To be alive is to face disruption. To be in love is to face the awesomeness of sharing one's life with another. To be a parent is to face the colossal challenges of raising children in a world where seductive distractions beckon from every screen and so much is beyond our control. To be an adult is to face aging parents, declining health, and a society and job market where youth is worshipped, and to feel crushing burdens and expectations. This all can leave us wondering whether there is any room in our lives for our own selves. Often, it seems like there isn't.

The twists, turns, and apparent loss of personal power result in unhappiness and frustration. The Russian writer Leo Tolstoy wrote, in the very first sentence of *Anna Karenina*, "All happy families are alike; each unhappy family is unhappy in its own way." Tolstoy was a literary genius, but he had only a third of it correct. He's right in that happy families are alike, but wrong in the implication that a happy family at Point A is still going to be a happy family at Point B. He is also off the mark in suggesting that unhappy families and unhappy people are each unhappy in their own way. We're not. The fact is, we're not so unique.

Do not misunderstand. We humans absolutely do not come out of the oven like a batch of identical peanut-butter cookies. Each of us is an individual. We've got our own DNA, our own histories, our own family and social contexts, our own conceptions of the Almighty, and our own stances on how to live our lives. Where we're not so special is in the kinds of problems and crises we face. Your problems do have some differences from those of your next-door-neighbor or your cousin halfway across the country. The cast of characters may be different; the set and setting vary. Yet when the superficial outer layers are peeled away, the core will look familiar to whoever is assessing.

There's a gift in this commonality. That gift is this: To solve life's problems, you don't need to reinvent the wheel or build a hammer from scratch. Instead, you need to learn the techniques to understand and respond to your circumstances, secure in the knowledge that there are answers. There are a couple of ways to do this. One way is the pricy way: Make an appointment with a therapist or coach who will sit with you, hold your emotional hand, and work through your upsets. If you get the right therapist or coach, this can be highly effective. However, you'll need a nice bank account balance to make it work.

The other way is to read this book.

Ours is a can-do, problem-solving society. People around the world marvel at the pragmatic and can-do American spirit. We've made an art form of defining problems, creating solutions, implementing the solution, and then reaping the rewards. Some examples?

In 1961, the United States was fearful that our enemy Russia was far ahead of us in rocket technology. President John F. Kennedy committed billions of dollars to beat the Russians and put a man on the moon by 1970. We created and implemented the solutions; our Neil Armstrong set foot on the moon in the summer of 1969.

There's an energy crisis in our country. We want to reduce our dependence on foreign oil. We've got oil and natural gas underground in the continental United States, but had no way to get it out with conventional drilling. We created and implemented a solution called "fracking" that extracts that oil. America will soon be a net energy exporter, instead of an importer.

Millions of Americans suffer from migraine headaches. For decades, there was no solution to this debilitating condition. Medical researchers did the research and found that migraines center on the sphenopalatine ganglion (SPG) nerve bundle behind the bridge of the nose. Other researchers created and implemented a patient-activated stimulator that activates that nerve bundle. Upward of seventy percent of migraine sufferers are helped by the new stimulator. American FDA approval seems assured.

It's the American way: Identify the problem. Analyze it until we understand it. Create a solution. Implement the solution. Solve the problem. On to the next one.

There's no doubt that it's a great protocol for putting men into space, getting oil out of the ground, and solving medical mysteries. Alas, it's a prescription for disaster for the kinds of issues that mark our personal lives, for our personal problems are ever-changing and ever-shifting.

Take aging parents. Sometimes the issues are financial. Sometimes the issues are interpersonal. Sometimes they are medical, and sometimes they are even spiritual. A solution that's right at Point A in their lives and our lives might be exactly the wrong solution at Point B, when circumstances have changed. You think you've got something worked out, and boom! A collapsing real-estate market, a turn for the worse in an illness, or even an argument that you're having with a sibling can make the problem of the aging parents erupt like a volcano.

This does not mean the problems are insoluble. They're not. What it does mean is that *problems that involve our emotions are qualitatively different from problems of science or engineering.* We need to address them in a different way. To be solved, they need to be reframed. Problems have less to do with their facts than with our responses. If we can improve our response, we can improve our life. Learning our own personal systems for framing our lives and then changing that framework is the key to a smoother, happier, more loving, and more successful existence. Negative frameworks need to go. Positive frameworks need to be reinforced.

There are several common negative frameworks through which we address life's problems, all of which get separate treatment in this book. There is the framework of *reenacting through fear and trauma.* There are problems where we feel manipulated and under the thumb of a real or imagined *oppressor.* There are *living quandaries,* where we look at our choices and see no way out. There are problems where *guilt and shame* is the lens through which we assess the situation. There is the common and seductive framework of *victimhood.* There are those of us for whom life seems to be a revolving carousel of *upsets and disagreements.* Finally, for many, life is lived within the framework of an *addiction or addictions,* whether the addicted person is oneself or a loved one. The chapters that follow examine each of these frameworks in turn.

Supreme Court Justice Lewis Powell famously said of pornography, "I know it when I see it." You will know which negative framework is your own when you read it. Once it's identified, and you understand it, you can do something about it – just like a flight to the moon, producing more energy, or even curing migraines. But the thing that will be fixed here is actually more personal, and therefore more important. It's nothing less than your future.

George Santayana wrote that those who do not learn from history tend to repeat it. The reason that happens is that we tend to experience the same categories of problems. Same game, different field; same game, different player. The filters of our existence create patterns that repeat, much like ripples in a pond. How long the pattern continues is up to us, thought we may not believe it. The same kinds of problems will echo through our lives until we learn their lessons, gain full understanding, or quit resisting reality.

As we have all heard before, *what we resist will persist*. Only in the acceptance of reality can we respond to it as it is and not as we would see it through our self-imposed filters. It is easy to get stuck, and unless we get unstuck, we are doomed to repeat the past. But that fate need not be permanent. If we ask the right questions, we can be free to live life – with its joys and sorrows, comedy and tragedy, wisdom and truth, love and loss, hopes and dreams – as it was intended to be lived. We all can do it. This book is the starting place toward living your reframed life.

THE FIRST NEGATIVE FRAME:
REENACTMENT OUT OF FEAR AND TRAUMA

I have a spectacular client named Cathy. She's in her late thirties, an attractive actress who earns her living doing commercials, television, and the occasional film. You'd never know by looking that she is the eldest of five children whose father was diagnosed with schizophrenia when Cathy was a little girl. In fact, Cathy was removed from her home and placed in foster care because her father tried to kill her mother. Before she was removed from the home, Cathy would physically insert herself between her mother and siblings and her father. She would take beatings for her sisters. Her father is now in prison.

Somehow, she pulled it together from these horrific beginnings to make a life for herself. She is a living testament to the human spirit. I'm often in awe of her. So many parts of her life are working. What isn't working, though, are Cathy's love relationships. She's on her third marriage. The first two guys were, by her own admission, losers. They were bums; violent like her father.

Her third marriage is different. By all accounts, he's a great guy. Jayson is a professional athlete. They met when they were filming a public-service commercial together. They've been married for a few years; when Cathy first came to see me, she wasa pregnant with their second child, not long after having adopted their first. It should have been a tremendously exciting and hopeful time for them.

However, Cathy didn't feel joy or positive excitement. Instead, she was emotionally distraught. Why? Jayson had recently revealed that he thought he was addicted to prescription painkillers. He'd started taking them to alleviate physical pain left over from his pro sports days. Now, he couldn't function without them. He had come to understand that he's dealing with an addiction, and was ready to deal with it.

Jayson asked with an open heart for Cathy's help. Part of Cathy responded with compassion and caring, but a larger part of her – a part she could not control – responded with fury and loathing. How dare Jayson bring his addiction into their marriage! How dare he put their children at risk! How dare he bring this behavior to her!

She started to scheme about ways to fix Jayson's addiction as if it were a solvable medical problem that needed a treatment protocol. Yet she found out that the more she treated Jayson as an object that should be "fixed," the worse they were getting along. The cure, it turned out, was as bad as the "disease."

Here's where Cathy was right: Jayson had brought an addiction into their relationship, and that addiction was undermining their relationship. Where she was wrong was in the way she was addressing it. The real issue she was dealing with was *not* just Jayson's addiction to painkillers. The real issue was that her response to the addiction was a *reenactment out of fear and trauma*. In her reenactment, Cathy's feelings about Jayson, her children, and his addiction were motivated by her own traumatic past. Her feelings were as much a reaction to that past as they were triggered by anything in her present life.

The addition of motherhood to the equation of her life had overwhelmed her. I told her that I suspected that it would overwhelm any of us. She was not weak in any way, but she couldn't add one more thing to her plate. Jayson's confession of his addiction was a surprise to Cathy and felt even worse – like a betrayal, as well as a reminder of her unstable childhood with a father who also concealed important truths.

It seemed to Cathy that her past was playing out all over again. I knew it wasn't, but to her, it seemed to be actually happening; this was where our real work began.

Cathy required a world that's under control. Anything for which she felt unprepared tripped an almost primal switch that sent her into survival mode. She disliked any surprises, changes, or unknowns. Any of these three triggers whipped her back to a past where she'd been less a person than a survivor.

Once we identified the source of her fear and trauma, she was able to place her emotions in context. We worked through her roller-coaster childhood memories. As we did, she began, for the first time in her life, to be conscious of her present emotions. Finally, she could see how she was collapsing two realities together, and how the reality of the past was mandating an overreaction to the reality of her present. With this insight, her love for Jayson and willingness to be his partner in his path to a drug-free life shone through. Most importantly, she was able to identify other parts of her life and history where fear and trauma drove her emotions and her actions, and even predict situations where she'd need to guard against letting the past smear the reality of the present.

THE SECOND NEGATIVE FRAME:
THE POWER OF YOUR OPPRESSOR

I magine this scene. It's a big Hollywood red-carpet event: the opening of a movie, the Grammy awards, or maybe even the Oscars. Limousines are pulling up; celebrities are getting out. The starlet *du jour* – it could be Scarlett Johansson, Jennifer Lawrence, or Halle Berry – gets out of her limo wearing an absolutely stunning gown by a designer like Elie Saab. (Google the one that Halle wore at the 2002 Academy Awards, if you want an example. It's dazzling.)

The crowds are screaming and the photographers are doing their thing as the starlet makes her way up the red carpet. VH1 and Bravo reporters rush to interview her. She's waving to the masses, her perfect teeth gleaming. The world seems to be eating out of her well-manicured hands. And then – it's hard to imagine it happening in front of an audience of a billion people like this – the starlet crashes to the ground in a heap. Her purse goes one way, her shoes go another, and her awesomely coiffed hair tumbles over her face. Meanwhile, a billion people around the planet are drawing the same awful conclusion. We can almost hear the exclamations, delivered in dozens of languages.

"What a klutz!"

"She's drunk!"

"She has to be on something!"

Aides rush to help her. She gathers her dignity and makes her way into the ceremony. But the damage is done. Her reputation is sullied forever. Every time that people think of her, they'll think she is unbalanced – if not mentally, then physically. But here's what they missed, and will never know: there was a tiny hole in the red carpet, and the starlet's gorgeous silver Manolo heel got caught in it. That's the only reason she wiped out.

Not that anyone cares. It's a much better story to attribute her indignity to a personal character flaw than to an outside force. In fact, a variation on this scene happened with Jennifer Lawrence at the 2013 Academy Awards. Fortunately for Lawrence, she had just been awarded the Oscar for Best Actress and was climbing stairs to the stage without the benefit of a handrail. We gave her the benefit of the doubt. If it had happened out there on the red carpet, she might not have been so fortunate.

Social psychologists call our willingness to attribute behavior to character instead of environment the Fundamental Attribution Error, and it comes into play all the time. Simply put, it's a lot easier to attribute a person's troubles to a flaw in his or her character than to an outside force. She's narcissistic! She's a user! She's a ditz! She's disorganized! She's an addict! She's lazy! She's a workaholic! The list of possible accusations goes on, and on, and on.

Why do we do this? One possible explanation is that it is easier for therapists, counselors, priests, rabbis, bishops, and others in the helping world to seek to change peoples' imagined character flaws than it is to change their world. But sometimes – maybe even often – the problem is not the intrinsic character of the person with whom they're working, but one or more aspects of that world. When a person is faced with an oppressive world, or an oppressive person in their life, it should not be a surprise that they react with behavior that is not necessarily in their own best interest.

The clearest example of this is to think back to our national nightmare of Vietnam. Hundreds of thousands of Americans served gallantly in the military in that Southeast Asian conflict. A large percentage of them came home addicted to the opiates, especially heroin, that were endemic to that part of the world. During that meat-grinder puzzlement of a war, many soldiers used heroin as a buffer against the meaningless horrors they had to live and fight every day. When they were there, they were hooked. When they came home, they got unhooked, despite the fact that heroin is highly addictive. They became drug addicts not because of some flaw of character, but because of an oppressive situation. Change the situation, and life can be lived according to your highest, best self.

Here is a basic truth: Not only can situations be oppressive, but people also can be oppressors. When we live with an oppressor in our life, whether that oppressor is actively or subtly oppressive, we view everything in life in terms of that oppressor. That oppression becomes the frame for our existence. It is like a giant medieval torture rack that twists and contorts us into positions that we would never put ourselves into if we had the choice.

The only thing that will get us back to normal is to get out of that blasted rack.

Who are these oppressors? They can be almost anyone. Sadly, they can be our mothers or fathers. Bosses are often oppressors. Spouses can be oppressors. Even our children can be oppressors. Grandparents and godparents – almost anyone in whom we place the core of our existence, and whose approval becomes essential for how we live, can be an oppressor. The common trait of all oppressors is that the oppressor is not interested in our ultimate happiness and best interest. The core of their existence is wrapped up in their oppression of us or others. They actually feed off our cycle of fortune and misfortune.

The German word *schadenfreude* means taking pleasure in someone else's misfortune. Oppressors don't merely take pleasure from our misfortune; they thrive on it. But they don't want us to have so much misfortune that we might shrivel and die. Instead, they want to keep us alive and in the frame of oppression. We need to be healthy enough to be of service to them, but unhealthy enough to feed their twisted emotional needs.

Oppressors invalidate us in a way that strikes at our very foundations. We can feel dumb and stupid around them. When we challenge them, they tend to have all the answers. When caught in an untruth, they will work their way of it, turning the tables in a verbal jiu-jitsu that makes us the oppressor and them the victim. It is hard to get an honest emotional response from an oppressor, though he or she may play-act beautifully. The oppressor sows doubt. We doubt them, we doubt ourselves. It is from this doubt and upset that they squeeze the "juice" on which they thrive. What is disempowering to us is empowering to them.

Here are some examples from my practice of people who were living their lives stuck in the frame of their oppressor.

I had a client named Marla who had just finished school at a famous New York City fashion institute. Her goal was to become a designer with her own clothing line, but she had come to me because she was in a great dilemma about her work. The fashion industry is notorious for sucking up young women and spitting them out, using and abusing them, and all in the interest of providing "valuable experience" as they work their way up in the business. It's also an arena known for impossible bosses. The experience of Anne Hathaway's character in *The Devil Wears Prada*, with the incomparable Meryl Streep playing her boss, Miranda Priestly, is iconic. And no wonder – Streep's character is a classic oppressor.

Back to Marla. She got off to a great start with the designer, whom we'll call Kym. Kym seemed to love Marla. Took her lunch. Took her to meetings. Had her sit in on interviews that Kym did with the kinds of magazine that Miranda Priestly would have edited. Marla was flying. She could see herself in three years as being Kym's official protégée, and in five years as having a line of clothes of her own, maybe in firm that was a subsidiary of Kym's.

However, things started to go downhill within a couple of months. Marla, who was never a drinker, began drinking several nights a week with her colleagues. Her sleep became erratic. She started to have a hard time keeping up with her regular exercise program. Some days, she'd come home from work raring to put on her running shoes and do the path along the river. Other days, she couldn't motivate. She reported to me that Kym had turned mercurial. Some days, her boss was as nice as could be. Other days, she was hypercritical. Once, Kym criticized her for an hour over the font that Marla had chosen for a document, even though the font was the one that had been set as the program's default. Another time, Kym praised an outfit that Marla wore to work. Three weeks later, Kym was critical of the same outfit. Marla didn't ask why. She was too cowed.

The longer that Marla worked there, the more her happiness came to be defined by Kym. When Kym was good to her, Marla had a good day. When Kym was critical, Marla had a bad day. When Kym had no emotional reaction to Marla, then Marla wondered what she was doing wrong to make herself invisible. Kym dominated Marla's thoughts and feelings. Marla lived her life wondering, "What would Kym think?"

When Marla returned home for Christmas break, she came to see me because she had become fundamentally unhappy. I was a little shocked. I'd met with her when she was a teen, before she embarked on her education. I'd encouraged that path. I had always admired her spunk and independence. The young woman before me now was neither spunky nor independent. She was, in a word, oppressed. When I suggested to her that the problem was not in her character but in her boss, I thought the insight would dazzle her. Instead, she scoffed. All her friends in the business had bosses like Kym. I asked whether everyone was having the same sleeping, eating, exercise, and mood problems that she was having. She had to admit they weren't – that she had friends who were doing just fine.

Then I asked her how long most people tended to stay at Kym's design house. Was there a lot of employee turnover?

That did it. Marla started to weep.

The answer was yes. Few of Kym's employees tended to stick around. In fact, Marla was hard-pressed to think of anyone who'd been at the firm longer than three years. At first, she'd thought it meant there would be an opening for her. If she could just prove herself indispensable to Kym, the fashion world would be her oyster. I pointed out gently that plenty of the people who had left the firm in less than three years must have had the same idea.

Marla didn't stay with Kym for long after that. She sent me an email within two months of her return to New York that she'd found another gig with a different designer. This new boss, she reported, was pretty normal. And Marla's life had returned to normal.

It is impossible to live normally when your lot is tied up with that of an oppressor.

Here's another example from my practice. I have this client, Cynthia. She's divorced and has three kids. She has a great job as an interior decorator, and the divorce was four years ago. Cynthia comes from a big, tight-knit family like you often find in mid-size cities where the children don't scatter to the four corners of the earth. She has two sisters who've struggled in their lives. They have a hard time finding and keeping jobs, men, and their heads on straight. With her parents ineffectual, Cynthia's role in the family has been to support these somewhat flailing adult sisters. It's something she did without complaint. She offered her time. She offered her money. She found peace when her sisters were peaceful; she became roiled when her sisters' lives were in turmoil. It was a roller coaster of an existence where Cynthia did not know how each day would go. It all depended on how her sisters were doing.

Cynthia had pretty much resigned herself to a life alone. Who was going to want to be with a single woman with three children?

Then, she met Thomas.

Thomas was a driven entrepreneur. He was divorced, like Cynthia, but had no kids. Thomas came to love her artistic spirit, her functionality, and her ability to listen. She loved his masculinity, his intellect, and his creativity. She loved how he would talk through his new business interests with her. She came to find those discussions much more rewarding than her usual interactions with her two sisters. Cynthia was happier with Thomas than she'd been in forever.

Thomas wanted to marry her. And that's when the problems with the sisters escalated. The sisters drove wedges between Cynthia and Thomas. They claimed that Cynthia's marriage to Thomas would be a betrayal of the family. Cynthia knew intellectually that this was false, but emotionally, their words struck home. The sisters even talked to Cynthia's children about Thomas, trying to turn the children against the relationship. They knew how much Cynthia cared about her kids, and how she would not bring a man into their life whom the kids didn't want, and so, they tried to make it so the kids wouldn't want Thomas. The sisters took Cynthia's children aside and tried to influence their thinking about Thomas.

When Cynthia came to see me, she was a wreck. She didn't know what to do. She felt caught between her own desires of herself and those of her family. The closer to Thomas she became, the worse her sisters seemed to be doing, and the more she felt responsible for their decline. She wanted to cut back on the amount of money she was sending to the sisters, but guilt prevented her from doing so. She wondered if there was something wrong with her in not being able to find balance amongst all these forces.

As I had with Marla, I tried to show Cynthia that there was nothing wrong with her. What was wrong was how her sisters were oppressing her. They seemed to have found new life and spirit in this effort to keep Cynthia and Thomas apart. It was almost like something from *Days of Our Lives*. It took several sessions to help Cynthia see that what her sisters were doing was not normal; that they were manipulating Cynthia emotionally, and that the emotional manipulation was not for Cynthia's benefit but for their own. Finally, Cynthia gave her sisters an ultimatum: Back off, or she would back away.

Like the Wizard of Oz behind the curtain, the sisters turned meek. They realized it was better to get the help that Cynthia was willing to offer on Cynthia's terms than to get no help at all. Now, Cynthia and Thomas are married.

There are pages and pages to be written on the psychology of oppressors. They can be sociopathic, bipolar, narcissistic, or have other recognized psychiatric disorders. We call them invalidators. Anti-social. Sharks. Human vampires. Parasites. Soul-suckers.

Their oppression can be active or passive. It can be outright manipulation, or be disguised to make it look as if it is in your best interest. Most of the time, oppressors do not even realize that they are oppressing. If they do, they justify it and rationalize it.

My point is not to diagnose and treat the oppressor. I leave that to their individual therapists or counselors. The point is for us to recognize that when there's an oppressor or oppressors in our lives, it is incumbent upon us to figure out who they are and then determine the best way to remove them entirely or mitigate their impact. If we don't, we're stuck on the torture rack. Sometimes the solution is the severance of our life from that of the oppressor, like what happened with Marla and her evil boss. Sometimes the solution is to redefine the relationship and hold to the redefinition, as with Cynthia and her sisters.

The alternative to extricating ourselves is bleak. We will live our lives stretched by the frame of our oppressors. The oppressors will define our moods, our activities, and even our sex lives. It will be as if we are living some strange perversion of a twelve-step program, where we admit that we are powerless over our lives and turn ourselves over to a Higher Power. However, this Higher Power is actually a Destructive Power, and we will be held in that Destructive Power's unholy embrace until we claw our way out. There is no alternative to our taking action; the oppressor is not going to do it for us – not when the ups and downs of our oppression fuel the fires of their oppressive lives.

I mentioned Miranda Priestly from *The Devil Wears Prada* as a classic oppressor. She is. But our films, novels, and stories are full of them. They make great villains. Some other great examples are Doc Holliday's girlfriend, Big Nose Kate, in the spectacular film *Tombstone*. If you recall, Holiday suffers from tuberculosis. He's supposed to stay out of the gambling parlors and beer halls to protect his fragile health. His closest friends remind him of this. Kate? She encourages his carousing, because the more ill he becomes, the more he must lean on her, and the more control she has over him.

There are more. Rollo Tomasi from *L.A. Confidential* is an oppressor. The prince who became a king in *Gladiator* is one, too. In the first season of the gripping Showtime series *Homeland*, there are actually two oppressors: The terrorist Abu Nazir, who saved Nicholas Brody's life while he was in captivity in Iraq, is an oppressor. For much of the series, Brody believed he owed his very existence to Nazir. To an extent, even, this is true. Were it not for Nazir's intervention after Brody was captured in Iraq, Brody knew, he would be dead. Brody came to love Nazir, though Nazir had a plan of his own, and Brody's life and happiness had nothing to do with that plan. Brody was simply another chess piece for Nazir to move. The other oppressor in the series was American Vice President William Walden. This is another man who had a plan of his own, the best interests of others around him be damned if they didn't serve his plan. Oppressors can be of every race, religion, and creed.

When oppressors take it too far, they can end up on the wrong end of the law. In 2013, there was a celebrated murder trial in Arizona involving a young woman named Jodi Arias who stood accused of shooting, stabbing, and practically decapitating ex-boyfriend Travis Alexander. It seems that most of Alexander's friends were suspicious of Arias, and even warned him to stay away from her. Yet her seduction was complete, and Alexander fell under her spell. She seemed pliable and conforming. Alexander was a Mormon; she joined his church. Alexander liked certain kinds of sex; Arias became an apparently willing participant in those sexual acts so that he could maintain a veneer of chastity. He lived in Arizona, she lived in northern California; she traveled days to visit with him. Finally, she even moved to his town.

This woman who appeared sweet and innocent on the outside was able to dominate him from the inside. She gained his trust and gained control in the process. Alexander thought he was getting a woman of sweetness, pure heart, and devotion to the same God whom he worshipped. In fact, he got a woman who lied to suit her purposes and who raged when Travis came to discern the truth of her character. The sweetness and innocence was a smokescreen that covered a heart incapable of love and compassion. Alas, his "a-ha" moment came too late.

Why would anyone fall under the spell of an oppressor, whether it be Abu Nazir, a designer like Kym, or Cynthia's sisters? They can be charismatic. They can offer something of value, but hide their true goal. Sometimes their true goal is not visible even to themselves – their oppression operates on an unconscious level. The relationship with our oppressor may even be functional for us for a time, until it turns oppressive. Once we are inside it, letting go is hard, and we even may feel like failures for doing so.

But let go we must. Without identifying the oppressors in our lives and understanding how it is that we are part of a symbiotic relationship with them, our lives will not change. I've never seen an addict of any kind who did not have an enabler in his or her life – an oppressor. The issue, though, goes way beyond addiction. It goes all the way to living a healthy, grounded, and envisioned life. A failure to let go means we're destined never to fulfill our potential, never to know peace, and never to know our sovereignty. It is no way to live. The frame of the oppressor is a frame that must be broken.

THE THIRD NEGATIVE FRAME:
QUANDARIES

We have all kinds of names for being faced with two choices that both have a strong negative outcome: Caught on the horns of a dilemma. Stuck between a rock and a hard place. Forced to pick the lesser of the two evils. Making a "Hobson's choice." Trapped between the devil and the deep blue Sea. Having no good alternative, no way out.

I prefer to call these situations what they are: quandaries.

What I've seen in my practice is that while life presents everyone with quandaries to an unfortunate degree of frequency, there are some people whose existence seems to be trapped in a frame of quandaries. That is, so many of the choices that they must make in their lives, whether about love, education, childrearing, money, and even faith, are shoehorned into what the great sex therapist David Schnarch calls a "two-choice dilemma," where there are two contradictory choices before the person, and the person wants both of them. Schnarch's most famous example of this is a marital partner who wants the other partner to initiate sex, but also wants to be the one who is directive of sex when it happens. Most of the time, the partner does nothing. When any movement is perceived to bring pain, the first instinct is to make no movement at all.

Remember the famous story of Aron Ralston, the experienced climber who found himself in a life-threatening quandary in 2003? Ralston, an accomplished mountaineer, was climbing in the slot canyons of southeastern Utah. Through a series of fluke events, his right arm became trapped by a dislodged boulder. Ralston was pinned, literally between a rock and a hard place. He'd told no one that he was venturing into the wild. He had no way to make a call, set off a flare, or otherwise contact civilization. At first, Ralston though that there was no way that he would survive. He was trapped for five days, rationing his food and water and planning for his own death even as he worked futilely to move the boulder and extricate himself.

Several days into his ordeal, a hungry and dehydrated Ralston had an epiphany that was also a quandary. He realized that if he could somehow cut off his own arm, he might be able to free himself. Of course, he'd be left sixty-five feet above the ground with a bleeding stump of a forearm. But at least he would be able to move.

Suffice it to say that Ralston today is a well-known motivational speaker without a full right forearm. He lost twenty-five percent of his blood and forty pounds during his ordeal. Yet he survived to tell his tale and motivate others to face their own quandaries, and he survived because he was willing to take an action and accept the painful consequences of that action. His story was made into the film *127 Hours*. It is a compelling tale of a heart-rending quandary.

Here are some other examples of quandaries I found poking around online for just a few minutes:

"Randall and Shawn were happily married until Shawn discovered men's magazines in her husband's bag. Now Randall is out of the closet as a gay man, and he's struggling to keep his family together. Shawn wants to know if they should stay married for their two preteen children or get a divorce. How are their kids handling the news that their father is gay?" *(From the online message boards of television personality Dr. Phil McGraw.)*

"I've been married twice. The first time was a love marriage and this time, it's like a typical [ethnic] arranged marriage. I've been living with my husband for more than two months now, away from his parents as well as mine. Now, the bone of contention between us is his mother, whom he wants me to obey and please. I have explained many a time that there's a limit to how much I can do. My husband too was married before and his previous marriage was destroyed mainly because of his mother's intervention. Now, I fear that he expects me to keep his mother with us forever." *(From the online message boards of the writer and thinker Deepak Chopra.)*

"My wife is angry with me because she thinks that I am too harsh with the kids when I discipline them. When my four year old is out of control, I will hit his behind. If my eight year old is shouting and won't shut up, I might swipe his bottom. I want the kids to know that I am in charge. I don't think it harms them to be lightly spanked. But my wife acts like I'm a Nazi war criminal. She says that I need to talk to the kids or send them to time-out. I do send them to time-out, but if they dawdle, I'll hit them. Then they go to time-out. Please advise me if you think my behavior is out of bounds. And what can I tell my wife so that she will be with me instead of against me?" *(From the message boards of www.wholefamily.com)*

The quandaries in these three examples are clear. In the one from Dr. Phil, the wife's dilemma is whether she should divorce Randall with all the carnage that will ensue for her and the children, or stay in the marriage with a gay (or at least bisexual) husband, which is nothing she ever bargained for. In the story from the Chopra boards, the woman is caught between the expectations of culture and her own expectations for happiness. In the last example, the father is caught between wanting to please his wife and his own expectations for childhood discipline.

In all three cases, the actors cannot have both. The interesting question is how long each of the people remained stuck between their rock and their hard place and simply did nothing, allowing the quandary to persist. Given the choice between getting cancer or quitting smoking, many of us will find a third way: We smoke another cigarette and put off the decision for the six minutes the cigarette is burning.

Here's the thing about all quandaries: a person stays stuck in the frame of it until it is resolved. If you're one of those people who tend to have a lot of quandaries in your life, this could be the negative frame into which you organize your life. Like Aron Ralston, your instinct is to not make a move to cut yourself out of your quandary, unless the situation is truly life and death. Even situations that feel like life and death become holding patterns, whether the issue is love, weight loss, sobriety, or whatever. It is safer to be trapped than to make a breakthrough, and there are ready and believable excuses for not getting unstuck. No one would have blamed Aron Ralston if he had died trapped by that rock.

I often see quandaries in the arena of extramarital affairs. I had a client named Gary who, on the outside, had a pretty enviable life. He was a stockbroker with a strong customer list, lived in a lovely home in Park City, Utah, and had three children (the youngest was five, the oldest was thirteen) and a wife whom everyone admired. However, Gary's feelings toward his wife had changed. He maintained – and I came to believe that he was telling me the truth – that he didn't love his wife anymore. Their sex life was nonexistent. He had gone outside the marriage for sex, but was not in love with anyone else. He felt awful about it. He was stuck in a quandary that's not too far from the one of the woman who discovered that her husband is gay. If he left his wife, he'd lose his kids. If he stayed in the family matrix, he'd feel like he was losing himself.

He didn't want to hurt his wife, he didn't want to hurt his kids, and yet, at the same time, he didn't want the status quo to continue. But he was unwilling to budge because of the pain it would cause. Most often, a man in Gary's situation does nothing, until somehow an outside force upsets the apple cart. In my experience, the cart *does* upset, eventually. It is amazing how an undeleted text message or email can reveal what a person is doing in their private or secret life.

While Gary's situation may read like a male cliché, it is not a male issue. It is a human issue. We women face the same thing in our marriages. We tend to be attracted to men in one of two ways: Either we spark to a guy's sexuality and heat, or we spark to their ability to provide. It's money or love; the provider or the lover. It is not unusual for a woman who chooses the provider over the lover to be bored erotically several years down the road into her marriage. It is similarly not unusual for the woman who chooses the lover over the provider to get sick of financial struggles. The quandary is what to do. In the first case, the woman feels the deprivation of her eroticism and sexuality. In the second case, the woman feels the deprivation of a decent place to live and a car that runs consistently. In both cases, the most common reaction is inertia – or an affair and inertia. The quandary persists until the cart is upset and some outside force shatters the frame. Unfortunately, the shattering tends to be emotionally violent.

It may seem like those who are caught in quandaries are the ultimate wimps. Those on the outside want to scream, "Do something! Make a choice! You can't go on like this forever!" What's particularly telling is that the people in these quandaries, morally bankrupt as they might be by conventional standards, have parts to their personalities that are actually very decent. They do not want to cause pain for others, and their drive not to cause pain becomes paramount. Therefore, everyone remains stuck – the person not doing the telling, and the others around him or her who are affected by the quandary-holder's deception.

Quandaries are not always about sex and romance. I see them a lot with body-image issues. There are women who will put on weight over the course of a relationship because it makes them less likely to cheat on their spouses. They feel that because they're heavier, others outside the marriage will come on to them less, and they will be less tempted by what the brilliant sex therapist Esther Perel calls the shadow of the third. Of course, adding weight does not normally make for a better erotic relationship with one's spouse, a better body image, or better health. We're thin while we're courting, and add weight during a marriage. We know it's crazy, yet we do it because it is a way to avoid causing pain to others. It is as if adding weight builds a fence around a potential sexual transgression.

I had a client named Phyllis. At the time I saw her, she was a classic pear-shaped woman – a willow from the waist up, and a planet from the waist down. Phyllis had had a horrendous childhood full of sexual abuse from a stepfather who had violated her under her skirts with his fingers. The stepfather never touched her above the waist, and her body, where he had touched her, had ballooned. She went to doctors to try to figure out why she was pear-shaped, but there was little that they could do. Bodies are bodies, and they can only be reshaped so much. What did happen was that once Phyllis discovered the frame of her quandary, she was able to reshape her body with a combination of exercise and some reasonable plastic surgery that augmented her breasts.

Another client with a quandary who came into my practice was a high-profile family where the father was involved in state politics and frequently mentioned in the news. His wife was a stay-at-home mom and a devout Catholic. They had three great children, the oldest of whom was seventeen-year-old Callie. They thought that things with the children were stable, until Callie revealed a pregnancy that she'd managed to keep secret for many months. They figured out that she was pregnant only at the start of her third trimester.

Some interrogation revealed that the father was Callie's boyfriend, a twenty-year-old named Zack, who similarly came from a conventionally successful family. Callie hid the pregnancy and protected Zack, but got no reciprocity from Zack. In fact, he had started rejecting her. Eventually, it came out that the sex might not have been wholly consensual between the two.

I came into this frame a couple of years after the baby was born. It was a maelstrom of quandaries. Callie was not equipped emotionally to raise the child. Zack's parents were making noises about adopting the toddler themselves. When Callie's parents caught wind of this, they moved to adopt the boy. Their wish was for Callie to attend college and make a life for herself. It would be an unconventional arrangement, but they thought it was making the best of a bad situation.

Callie's parents adopted the baby. I started working with Callie when she was a student at a major university. She was one of those people who tried to fill her life with productivity. I could see that she was consumed with staying busy so she that could stave off the looming void that came with her parents raising her child. She would travel home and spend time with her parents and her son. It was awkward and painful for her and for her parents as well, as they did not want Callie to be too close to her own boy. They feared that a close relationship with Callie would interfere with the child's attachment to them as parents.

I had never seen so many quandaries in one place before. The dad didn't want the rapist family to have the baby, so he fought for adoption, though he knew the impact this might have on Callie. Callie's mom wanted her daughter to make something out of her life, yet secretly resented being stuck with a baby at midlife. Callie was in her own quandary. She wanted to mother her own child, but knew she was not equipped to do so. At the same time, there was a powerful natural mother-daughter bond with her own baby. Unpacking these quandaries was like working through a Gordian knot without an opposable thumb.

Ultimately, Callie became the mother to her own child. It was a peculiar adoption proceeding, but the judge saw the wisdom of it.

Quandaries arise all the time with drugs and alcohol. My own father was an outstanding young baseball player. Major league material, really. Yet he fell in love, married young, and then had to support a young family. He was so psychologically frustrated that he never got to push his athletic talent as far as it could go. It must have been devastating to him. His choice of response, though, was devastating to those around him. He started drinking, and he pretty much never stopped. Then, his quandary was whether to stop the drinking and face the pain of disappointment, or continue the drinking and face the pain his drinking caused his family. Part of that quandary was that he was afraid of how he would be with others if he didn't drink, and had to confront his own monumental disappointment with his own life.

A person living inside the frame of quandary is living a life caught in amber of his or her own making. But that life in amber is not something that the person in the quandary wants to live. Those who are caught in quandaries tend to be gentle, non-aggressive, even kind people. They are not out to create strife, and in fact tend to back away from it. Others around them may have high expectations for them, and they do not want to let them down. Others' happiness may depend on their own stability – or at least their outward stability. They may be around others who would flat-out disown them if they went public with their quandary. They may be used to living under the harsh judgment of others. They make a calculation: It is less painful to live inside the quandary than to make that quandary public.

It is important to underscore that a reasonable number of quandaries is part of life. We all will face unpleasant dilemmas. An aging parent may fall and break hip while we live a thousand miles away and there is no local relative to take the lead on bringing the parent back to health. We may have jobs and lives far away, and our parent may even have encouraged us to take these paths. The issue of the ailing parent, though, is real.

The difference between these "normal" quandaries and a life bounded by an unending frame of quandaries is that the quandary of the ailing parent is temporary. There will be an outcome to it. The problematic quandaries are the ones that could potentially last a lifetime. The status quo of the quandary could go on forever until the truth comes out. As I said, usually it does come out. The unconscious mind is a powerful thing. It may well want to resolve the quandary even when the conscious mind is trying to protect the status quo.

How does one resolve a quandary in a healthy way, as opposed to an unconscious, destructive way? The solution most often lies in the person caught in that quandary being willing to take on the suffering of that quandary's resolution. It may involve going over and over through the options until one looks better than another.

Most often, though, it comes in our taking responsibility for our actions and being willing to frame our lives not in terms of quandaries, but in terms of necessary losses. We need to be willing to take the heat and understand that heat is natural. We need to face the fire and tell the truth. There is more pain in the withholding than in the sharing. In David Schnarch's terms, we choose one of the things that we want, and choose the pain of not having the other.

There tend to be two opposing intentions in all quandaries. They are dichotomies of opposing intentions. For example, there may be a dichotomy of public honor and personal self-expression or even self-preservation. We see this often with politicians who go astray and people who have secret affairs. There may the quandary of stability versus instability, or the quandary of safety versus loss. In fact, loss comes up again and again in quandaries. We who tend to have a lot of quandaries tend to protect ourselves against loss, particularly losses that challenge a personal value system. We fear we will lose our honor, our finances, our children, our self-respect, our future. We fear a self-image of ourselves as the bad guy.

Alas, loss is inevitable. For everything we gain, there's something lost.

I think of a family in my practice who had an adult child living at home. Jodi is an adult woman who is severely handicapped. Not the cutesy, let's-celebrate-her-on-a-TV-show kind of handicapped, but the gritty, difficult kind of handicapped where keeping the adult child clean, safe, and comfortable is sucking away at the family's life. Her body is mature. She has the regular cycles of a female but the mental capacity of a two-year-old, with a healthy measure of autism thrown in to boot. If one can imagine a person caught in the "Terrible Twos" for life, Jodi is that person.

The quandary is clear: does the family institutionalize the adult child, or continue to suffer? The dilemma is profound. It cuts to honor, religion, self-respect, public image, and the future. This was one of the most painful cases I've ever worked through with a couple. They were vibrant, lively people. They loved to hunt, camp, and travel. That's who they were, and they tried to maintain that vibrancy as their daughter aged into adulthood. Unfortunately, the older she got, the more difficult and soul-consuming she became to manage. She was beyond their expertise, but they did not want to abandon their daughter, and they saw long-term care facilities as abandonment. Finally, once the husband and wife reached their sixties, this family placed the daughter in a nearby facility. They see her often. But they can also live their lives. Something gained, and something lost.

Quandaries may not have beautiful outcomes. Often, they don't. But facing them head-on and refusing to filter your life into quandaries when it's not absolutely necessary to do so is one of the keys to living a full, vibrant, loving, honest, and open life.

THE FOURTH NEGATIVE FRAME:
VICTIMHOOD

Picture, if you will, a "perfect" state of being. Everyone is inclined to like you. You are always justified in your position. Nobody ever doubts your sadness or wonders whether your anger is justified. How you act toward other people makes less of a difference in how they respond to you than it should – you always get the benefit of the doubt. Others are solicitous to a fault, and forgiving even when you wonder yourself whether you deserve to be.

Sound good? There's more. When something bad happens, even if it happens on your watch, it is never going to be seen as your fault. There is always going to be an outside reason, blame placed elsewhere, and sympathy extended to you for having the bad luck to be in the middle of an unpleasant situation. When bad things happen to you, you are never a contributing factor. Everyone feels sympathetic to you, even empathetic. Whatever the reason you put forward for your difficulties, people will believe you.

Not a bad way to be, huh?

Not bad at all, except for the catch: However you are in your life cannot and will not change for the better so long as you maintain that state of being. You will not form closer relationships with others, including your parents, spouse, and children. You will most likely not progress in your career. You won't move to another place because your life and this "perfect" state depends on the status quo being maintained. Nor will you have the freedom to look at the world, your life, your God, and your future any differently from how you are looking at it now, because it could well upset the apple cart of your "perfect" state of being.

There is a name for this "perfect" state of being. It's victimhood. It is also the fourth major frame to which people affix their lives. In some ways, it's the most dangerous of them all, because it is so darn seductive. There is scarcely a person alive who can always resist being seduced into a victim mentality. The rewards in the here and now are just too tempting. There is much short-term gain and not much short-term pain. The pain of victimhood tends to be further down the paths of our lives, in the roads not taken and the vistas not experienced. It is the pain of living a life narrowly instead of fully, and of not becoming our highest and best selves. It is the pain of being stuck instead of moving forward with our lives, and living to the maximum. Victimhood is the one frame to life that no one will ever blame you for adapting, but also the frame that is most constrictive.

Before we go any further, I want to say something important and underline it: <u>There are people who are indeed victims</u>. Let me repeat that in italics and underscored, in case a text message came in at the exact same time that you were reading those words. <u>*There are people who are indeed victims*</u>. There are people who have faced massive and significant traumas in their life, traumas that any of us would shudder at the idea of experiencing because they are so far beyond the pale of normal human experience as to shock the conscience. One can think of the great writer and thinker Viktor Frankl, who survived the Nazi death camps. Or Elie Wiesel, who did the same. By a more contemporary measure, we grieve for those wounded in senseless shootings, and the families who have lost loved ones to tragic violence. It might be better to think of these people as Victims with a capital V, to distinguish their experience from the smaller-scale victimizations that the rest of us face in our everyday lives. It is worth pointing out, too, that Frankl and Wiesel, and so many others, made a radical choice about their own experiences: They owned and own it. They understood and understand what an important part of their lives it has been. But they do not let themselves be controlled by it. If any proof of this is needed, look at the kinds of lives those men led after the horrors of their youth. Frankl wrote paradigm-changing books, and Wiesel won the Nobel Peace Prize.

Part of the reality of the negative frame of victimhood is that we live in a society that is, by its very nature, emotionally generous. Generosity of spirit is one of the best things about America. We are taught to be giving to others. Empathy for feelings and sympathy for pain is seen as a positive. We are also taught to extend this kindness beyond those that we know to those whom we see. Americans give more money to charitable causes than any other people on the face of the earth. We do it whether we are liberal or conservative, poor or rich, Christian, Jew, Muslim, Hindu, or atheist. We have a particular skill for joining together as a community to support those in pain. There is no more heartwarming and pride-inducing example of this than the way the nation joined to support the victims of September 11, 2001. We know how to do this, we like to do this, we feel good about ourselves when we do this, and we get a lot of community support when we do this. It is part and parcel of being an American. When a tidal wave strikes halfway around the world, it is the American military that rushes to the rescue. We have been known to help victims of natural disasters in countries that hate us. At least we offer the help. It is a gloriously American characteristic.

This generosity, though, can be tempting – even too tempting – for the recipient. A few examples of how the frame of victimization works for us and against us at the same time are useful.

There was a man in my practice named Zeke. He did the whole happily married thing with a great woman, named Teri. They had been married for twenty years, built a life together, bought a house and a vacation house in Palm Springs, California, and were now in their mid-forties. It was the prime of their lives. Zeke's work as a real-estate investor and developer was paying off in a big way. Teri worked with Zeke in his office, answering phones and the like, but actually had primary child-rearing responsibility for three kids. One was off to college in Texas, and the other two were in high school and middle school, respectively.

Everything seemed great – except it wasn't. Teri and Zeke didn't have much of a sex life, but the fact is that, sadly, the majority of people over the age of forty-five don't have much of a sex life. Zeke and Teri chalked up their lack of a sex life to stress and "normal" dwindling of libido. (This "dwindling" may be culturally accepted, but it is not inevitable. We'll talk about it later in the book).

What was really happening with Teri and Zeke was that Teri wasn't being upfront about her sexuality with Zeke. She called herself hetero, but as the marriage progressed, she found herself in a secret affair with a woman we'll call Alana. Alana was in a parallel situation to Teri – also married, but coming to understand that her sexuality was veering toward attraction to women only.

When the eldest of Teri and Zeke's children came home from college to announce to Teri and Zeke that he was gay, Teri took the cue. Not all that long afterward, Teri came out to Zeke: She was also gay, and she wanted an arrangement where she could see Alana openly. After all, she argued, it wasn't as if she and Zeke were tearing up the bedsheets with passion.

Zeke went nuts, especially when he found out that if they divorced, he was going to have to pay alimony based on their long relationship, and Teri would have a substantial interest in his burgeoning real-estate holdings because of the community property laws in their state. He felt incredibly victimized; he railed against twenty years of victimization. It was completely unfair, he felt, that Teri was going to take his money after she took the best years of his life. All his friends were sympathetic, turning against Teri and supporting him. His children were similarly sympathetic, including the son who had come out as gay. The son said that the mother should have been honest long before and had no right to have duped Zeke.

It took several in-depth conversations with Zeke to point out that he now had choices for his life that he hadn't had before the revelation. He could, if he chose, continue to live in a world that had gone sour. He would get a good deal of social support if he continued in that world.

Or, he could move onto newer horizons. I pointed out that while Teri had an interest in his past businesses and there was nothing he could do about that, she would have no interest in any new businesses that he started. Perhaps his efforts would be better spent on things that were fresh. Perhaps, in a divorce settlement, she might take a larger lump sum in exchange for giving up some of those ongoing business interests. It had been known to happen.

At the end of our time together, Zeke came to me with some stunning revelations of his own. He brought up how he might well have colluded in Teri's secrecy. Not on purpose, but subconsciously. Her time away from home with Alana served him, in its own way. He accepted Teri's role in the marriage; there was even underlying sadness in his voice as he spoke. Yes, Teri had taken advantage of him. But really, all he could do was learn from the experience and move forward. He was ready to stop viewing life as if it were framed by victimhood.

Another example of the frame of victimhood is with grownups who are the victims of physical, sexual, or emotional abuse as children. Let me say first that there is never an excuse for an adult to engage in this kind of behavior. It is always despicable as well as often criminal. It happens more often than we care to admit, and even in "good" families. It is hard for a child whose father or mother hit him or her as part of their discipline to not do the same thing when they reach adulthood. It takes a real force of will not to repeat the same kind of conduct, even knowing how it feels to be the victim of that kind of abuse.

However, the fact of the abusive upbringing and abusive parent or parents can grow to dominate a person. Carlotta was a beautiful young woman in my practice. She was in her late twenties, smart as can be, and with a wonderful soul. Yet she could not keep a job for more than a few months before she'd be fired, mostly for not carrying out her duties the way that her supervisors wanted her to. It was almost as if she were providing an excuse for the supervisors to victimize her. Carlotta always had a ready reason for why the supervisors were being unfair; it was hard to argue with her logic. But it was also hard for her to argue with the depressing and limiting facts of her life. She hadn't had a real boyfriend since she was at junior college, she was still living with roommates, and she had made no moves at all toward a career. This wouldn't be too bad in theory, if Carlotta didn't want more. The thing is, she did want more. She saw herself one day with a loving husband, a family, a home of her own, and work that she not only didn't get fired from, but also wanted to do.

Through the time that I was seeing her, Carlotta remained fixated on the abuse that she had suffered as a girl at the hands of both her father and mother. Carlotta had read all kinds of material on how being victimized as a child can damage a person for life, and she put herself forward as Exhibit A. It was difficult, and insulting, to argue with her logic about how she had been damaged by this conduct. Nor was there any possibility of her confronting her abusers as a way of moving forward—her parents had both passed away.

Carlotta had a strong support system. I've almost never seen a person so attached to her friends. She got plenty of sympathy from them; they were happy to be the wind beneath her wings. Probably, they felt great about helping her. She had even seen a psychotherapist who had treated Carlotta with respect, and was a wonderful listener and sympathizer, though Carlotta finished the therapy without any discernible forward progress. Between the friends and the therapist, it was a perfect system where everyone got what they wanted. Carlotta got sympathy. The friends got the satisfaction of supporting someone who was hurt. The therapist got paid and felt good about herself. Carlotta? She remained stuck.

Carlotta had a choice. She could dwell in the cave of her victimhood, or take what happened to her, give it a narrative and interpretation that added to her own power, and step into the sunshine. Ultimately, in our work, that's what I helped Carlotta to do. We worked hard to reframe the past and unframe the present. Carlotta found it helpful to understand her childhood and adolescence in terms of how she could muster the inner strength to survive and move on. She took heart from other victims who have moved on in their lives – victims whose travails were far more intense than her own. When Carlotta could separate her trauma from herself, her life started to change for the better.

Let me repeat again that no one should judge the depth of the traumas that are faced in life. All of us face traumas differently, and all of us face different kinds of traumas. How we face them is part psychological and part biological. What is a capital "T" Trauma for one person, which makes them a capital "V" Victim, is to another person a manageable trauma of which they are the kind of victims which they can accept, process, and move on. There is always going to be a certain percentage of truly damaged people on the planet; people who have been victimized terribly and whose lives are stained by the forces of brutality, hatred, cruelty, and just plain evil. Yet for the rest of us, the conscious choice to refuse to limit our lives in the negative frame of victimhood can mean liberation from a past that, by its very nature, cannot be changed. As our parents always told us, "What's done is done." What isn't done is what happens next.

THE FIFTH NEGATIVE FRAME:
UPSETS AND DISAGREEMENTS

The Jewish Talmud, that great compendium of law and teaching compiled by rabbis more than fifteen hundred years ago, has much to teach about the fifth frame in which the canvas of our lives is stretched: the frame of upsets and disagreements. In the section called *Pirkei Avot*, "Teachings of the Fathers," the sages of old discussed the four basic ways that people approach the world. "There are four types of temperaments," the Talmud instructs. "One who is quick to become angry and quick to calm down – his gain is outweighed by his loss. One who is slow to become angry and slow to calm down – his loss is outweighed by his gain. One who is slow to become angry and quick to calm down is pious. One who is quick to become angry and slow to calm down is wicked."

The rabbis were correct. There is almost nothing that can knock a person off his or her game like getting upset, except maybe for the experience of disagreement. Often, they go hand in hand, like an emotional peanut butter and jelly sandwich. Upsets range from small dismays to murderous rages. Disagreements range from being merely miffed to white-hot fury. None of us is immune. The best that we can hope for is some degree of peace. Most of the time, even that seems hard to attain.

The great comedian Louis C.K. talks about how he can be a perfectly nice guy most of the time, but when he gets behind the wheel of his car, he's transformed into some kind of anger-spewing beast. He finds himself flinging profanities and invective against the driver who drifted into his lane for a half-second and drifted out again, with no harm done. He admits he screams things that will never be heard from the safety of the driver's seat in a way that he would never scream them to someone in an elevator next to him. He's upset.

The rest of us have done the same thing at one time or another. The good thing about this kind of anger is that it does dissipate. In fact, it dissipates quickly. Road rage is called "road rage," not "road-plus-later-rage." In a strange way, we managed to compartmentalize that anger, let it fly, and then let it go. Few would find fault with this.

The problems start when we start letting disagreements and anger dominate us when we're not stuck in our cars. Very often, upset follows disagreement. I had a client come in recently to recount in excruciating detail the conversational blow-by-blow of a discussion – if you could call it that – she'd had with her husband of five years. Let's call her Cassie, and him Chris. They are, from the outside, a solid and privileged couple. They spend the months of April through October in North Carolina and come to Utah to ski in the winter. They're not Trump rich or Gates rich, but money is no issue at all in their marriage. Chris is a freelance writer for various outdoor magazines and has passive income from a family trust. Cassie made a small fortune through an online cosmetics business that is under the management of others but still provides her with an income stream. They're also childless by choice, have made it into their early forties in good health, and have no one in their families who's in jail or a cemetery.

I know. I had the same thought. What in the world could this couple be having a knock-down, drag-out fight about? Would that the rest of us had such easy lives!

It turned out that their argument was about Christmas. Mind you, they were in my office in March. Here was the story: For the first four years of their marriage, the two of them had gone to Chris' parents in Texas for Thanksgiving, and to Cassie's parents in Pennsylvania for Christmas. Chris had proposed that they change it up for the upcoming year, since his family had asked that they spend Christmas in Texas. Chris seemed to think it was a good idea and said yes without consulting Cassie.

Well, the Fourth of July fireworks offered little competition to how Chris and Cassie got into it over this. Cassie was furious about the fact that Chris didn't consult her, as well as that he had been willing to change the status quo. Chris alternated between equal irritation that Cassie always assumed she had a lock on their holiday arrangements, and bemusement that something as simple as switching dates for family visits would set off such an imbroglio. Cassie didn't find her partner's grinning one bit funny. She kept wanting Chris to apologize, but Chris didn't think he had anything to apologize for, really. He was sorry that he hadn't consulted Cassie, but pointed out that Cassie made unilateral decisions all the time that never caused an argument. He finally said that if Cassie wanted to go to her mom and dad's for Christmas it was fine with him. She just shouldn't expect that he would be there, too. This pronouncement ignited a whole other round of not-very-constructive engagement.

As a result of this dispute, Cassie found herself in a deep depression. It's not surprising. Depression and sadness follow upset and hostility like night follows day. In fact, it's fair to say that depression and sadness are the inevitable result of anger and hostility that remains unresolved…but not for the reasons that conventionally get offered. It's not because the upset and hostility somehow eat away at us and transform into depression the way that acid eats at a piece of metal. It's something else. It's that depression represents one of two types of failure. Either it represents a failed intention in your life, or a failed dream of yours. Or both. In Cassie's case, she had a couple of dreams that she held close to her heart. The first dream was a holiday dream. The idea of spending the Christmas holidays with her parents had special, sentimental significance. Who are any of us to dispute sentiment? Surely not me. In fact, if someone were to ask me what should be rescued from a burning building, a diamond ring or a box of family photos that can't be replaced, I vote for the photographs every day of the week. That vision of Christmas with her mom and dad, siblings, nieces, and nephews was a dream of Cassie's; a dream she was able to make come true every Christmas. Now, along came her husband, of all people, to wreck it – at least that's how she saw it. No wonder she was depressed. She had both a failed intention and a failed dream. And darn it, she was not going to let them go.

As a society, we do far better with depression than we do with upset and disagreement. At least, we think we do. Any of us can go to our family physicians – one does not even have to visit a psychiatrist! – and get a prescription for Lexapro, Celexa, or any of the SSRI antidepressants that have changed psychopharmacology so much in our lifetime. We have labeled depression a chronic medical and physiological problem, and to a certain extent, that is what it is. Ongoing states of upset and disagreement can't be sustained. They're too draining. So they morph physiologically into depression, which affects our serotonin, dopamine, and a whole slew of other hormones and brain chemicals. Do not get me wrong: there is a whole subset of people out there with severe chemical imbalances in their systems. Those people need medication, and need it fast. But for the rest of us, the depression that has us asking our doctors for the same scrips as our friends and neighbors, which are the same scrips we see advertised in magazines or on television, has its roots in a boulevard of broken dreams and failed intentions.

The great psychologist Dr. Fred Luskin likens the state of upset to a state of righteous indignation. He takes it one step further, in fact, by suggesting that there are times when we drift into tantrum. After all, what is a tantrum but a strong reaction to having someone act in a way that you don't want them to act, or for circumstances to turn in a direction that you don't want them to turn? And in both cases, there's not a darn thing that can be done about them.

To circle back to my clients Cassie and Chris, for better or for worse, Chris was being unmovable. I had sympathy for Cassie; he was being inflexible, for sure. But he also was not standing on ceremony. He was very clear about Cassie's option to go and have her Christmas with her family. Apparently, he would not hold that against her.

Cassie's upset had a tantrum-like quality to it. Not that she was prone on my floor kicking and screaming – hardly. This was a bright, accomplished, and interesting woman. The tantrum was more in her unwillingness to budge from the way she was framing the current problem between her and her husband; her unwillingness to accept that there might be different ways to give it meaning. I was more than ready to say that one of the ways to give it meaning was to acknowledge that her husband was, on this subject, being something of a jerk. Most husbands can be jerks, at one moment or another.

There was a way out for Cassie, for Chris (because his time of upset and disagreement is coming, surely!), and for the rest of us. It does not require a ceding of moral high ground, or our own selves, or even the righteousness of our beliefs. It has to do with keeping focus in our conversations on two things. The way out is our listening carefully, with as little judgment of what is being heard as possible. The moment we start judging is the moment we're enmeshed in our own emotional process. And the moment we're enmeshed in our own emotional process is the moment we're splitting our attention away from the person who's talking to us. It's axiomatic that we only have one hundred percent attention to focus at any one time. When we talk, we'd like that the people to whom we're talking give us one hundred percent of their focus. Neither they nor we can accomplish that feat if we're letting waves of emotion roll through us. Listen first. Listen all the way. Process. Consider. Only afterward can we find the space to react.

When I was a student, I constantly felt the urge to interrupt my own teachers, interjecting my own thoughts and analyses. Finally, the very best of them shared a basic truth with me: A person can't learn anything while the person is talking.

The second part – and this is pretty easy, if you've been listening carefully and without judgment – is to assure the person to whom you're listening that they are seen and heard. That means putting yourself in their shoes, looking at things from their perspective, and accepting that their point of view might well be different from yours. There is practically nothing more reassuring as an adult than to be seen and heard, and practically nothing less affirming than to be dismissed or overlooked. If the reason that a person is holding onto upset and reliving a disagreement is that the person feels they have not been seen and heard, I often feel like they've got a legitimate reason to be temporarily upset. After that, though, it becomes counterproductive. How do we know when it is counterproductive? When that upset keeps a person stuck in a tantrum or devolves into lingering sadness and depression.

My tongue is firmly in my cheek as I write this, but agreement is overrated. It is not hard to be friends with people with whom you disagree, and it can even be refreshing. Connection between people happens at a different level from politics, or what restaurant to eat at, or even where to spend the Christmas holidays. Couples connect on many different levels, from emotional to spiritual to sexual. It is too much to expect one hundred percent niceness one hundred percent of the time, as well as one hundred percent agreement. A hundred percent agreement only happens in the movies.

When I was growing up, I had a grandfather who was a bit of a sonofabitch. I mean it. The guy was never nice. I had chores that I had to do with him. I can remember him driving his tractor and glaring at me working. A smile was too much to hope for. If I got a nod from him, that meant the world. I wouldn't recommend my grandfather's approach as a way to win friends and influence people in a marriage, but I learned how to take meaning from my experience with him, and how to see and hear him on his own terms. Granted, my grandfather did not teach me much about communication and compassion – I'd be the first to say that. But what I did learn from him was a work ethic that has stood me in good stead my entire life. He taught me to have a thick skin. He taught me to rely on my own assessment of a situation and not depend on the approval of others in making my own judgments.

There were times that he upset me a lot, but ultimately, he taught me that the people who upset us the most are our best trainers. I'm not saying that we should marry people who are like my grandfather. Just learn from them.

I had a client named Denise who was locked inside the framework of anger and disagreement with another woman. The story is long and emotionally bloody. Denise was a successful hairdresser; Angie came to her as a client. She stayed as a client, and as hairdressers and clients do, the two women became friends and confidantes. They discovered that they came from similar backgrounds, and that neither of them had sisters. Each had young children of the same age, and their husbands were both police officers on the same large municipal force, though the husbands didn't know each other before Denise and Angie became friends. Soon, the guys became buddies. Let's call Denise's husband Gary and Angie's husband Reed. Believe me – no one in this story wants his or her real name used.

The two families got close. The couples double-dated. They had their kids over for sleepovers. The two women were like sisters, which felt like a heavenly gift, since both of them only had brothers. The families spent holidays together, cheered on the youth-soccer sidelines together, and vacationed together to places like Mexico and the Dominican Republic.

Then Angie started a secret affair with Denise's husband. The affair went on behind Denise's back for more than a year. Denise had no idea. Angie's husband had no idea. Gary and Angie were masterful at covering their tracks. At some point, Reed got suspicious. He knew many private detectives from his work on the force, and engaged one of them to follow his wife. He hoped against hope that the detective would have nothing to report. Unfortunately for the cause of fidelity, the detective followed Angie and Gary to a mall at the south end of the city. He took photographs of them eating lunch together in the food court, and then a short video of them holding hands on their way back to Gary's squad car. And then, video of the kissing by the car.

Reed confronted Angie by pretending to show her a funny YouTube video, but instead played the video that contained the private detective's material. Angie was busted.

She burst into tears. "What are we going to do?"

Reed said "We? You mean you. What are you going to do? You're out of here!"

He made Angie leave their home; she took their daughters with her. Angie decided to go – yes, I couldn't make this up – to Denise and Gary's house. She claimed to her best friend Denise that Reed had dumped her for no good reason, and that she had nowhere else to go. Reed didn't know that this was Angie's destination. He'd assumed that she'd gone to her mother's place across town. Denise wasn't going to contact him, and Gary sure wasn't going to contact him. Meanwhile, Angie and Gary were able to carry on their affair.

Let me just break in here and say that the logical thing here would have been for Angie to come to her senses, realize how much she had hurt Reed and her family life, and return to him pleading temporary insanity. As the kids say, that's not how it went down. Instead, Angie told Denise not to speak to Reed; that Reed was threatening herself and her girls. As for what was actually happening, Angie and Gary were planning their escape. And escape they did, in the dark of night, running away to Idaho together with all the children.

For Angie and Reed to fight this, they would have had to travel to Idaho and avail themselves of that state's court system. There were two more soap opera wrinkles. First, Denise caught her husband and Angie in an intimate moment not long before their departure. Second, Angie was pregnant by Gary. They told no one.

The situation worsened. Reed filed for divorce. So did Denise. Both were devastated beyond comprehension.

By the time Denise came to me, her ex and Angie had been living together in Idaho for nearly two decades. The divorces were ugly. The judges worked valiantly to straighten out the child-custody arrangements, but the upshot was that Reed's daughters were forced to refer to Gary as "Daddy" and to treat Angie and Gary's baby as if he was their natural brother. Gary turned out to be abusive, but Reed's best efforts to bring his children home were thwarted in the courts. His own children, so poisoned by the years with Gary and Angie, lied to investigators and would not testify adequately on their own behalf. This is beside the fact that their medical evaluations revealed anxiety and depression, as well as drugs to treat each of these conditions in their bloodstreams.

The story of the girls does not get better. They skid through school and barely graduate from high school. They don't even learn to drive until they are nearly twenty. Their foci are shopping and primping, much like Angie. Worst of all, maturity does not bring insight. Their fealty remains with Gary. They tell Reed that, "We owe our dad Gary. He has done so much for us."

Reed is completely powerless to stop this insanity. The man in him wants nothing more than to beat the crap out of Gary, but if he does that, he loses his career. The temptation is there nonetheless. On the other side of the equation, Denise's fury at Angie for wrecking her life and her relationship knows no bounds. For years, these two women have been locked in a long-distance mutual death lock. There is a *Les Miserables* quality to the obsession and anger. Denise posts her story online at any number of websites that are happy to host it. She writes letters to all the police officers in Gary's town letting them know who Gary really is and how abusive he has been to her and her children. When she has the children, she has to invoke the power of the state to collect child support because Gary does not willingly pay. She is the subject of mockery and gossip between Angie and her Idaho friends.

I came to this story when Reed became my client. When he first came to my office, he was a broken man. In the best tradition of men, he looked first to himself for the responsibility for this unholy mess, and then to the others involved. It seemed impossible to me that he would have the valor to do that, but that is fundamentally the kind of man he is. I would say, to their credit, that many men would do the same thing. They are less likely to ascribe blame than to accept it.

My work with Reed, then, was to reframe. Yes, he should be looking at himself, but in the way that a ship's pilot assesses the condition of his own vessel after a storm, instead of blaming the ship for the storm. There were so many gaping wounds in Reed's life that needed to heal. I wanted Reed to focus on healing those wounds. I also wanted him to stop blaming himself when blame was inappropriate.

It took him quite a while to get to that place, but he got there. Our work together, and time, helped to heal Reed. He accepted that the story might not have a happy ending on all fronts. He went on to meet a wonderful woman, married her, and is happier than he has ever been, save for the anguish of what is happening with his daughters.

Denise has never remarried. She has not been able to stop her suffering. Here it is, two decades after the first skirmish, and the war with Angie continues. She would say with some pride, in fact, that she hates Angie.

Women, it seems, are particularly prone to this kind of hatred and loathing. How they manifest their anger and disagreement at the objects of their anger boggles the mind, sometimes. Men, too, bear grudges, but it seems like there is some sort of masculine code of honor that governs the way that they fight. Remember that Reed in the story managed to resist his justified urge to physically attack Gary. Women have no such code. I had a client tell me – she was both ashamed and proud of this – that she once took a pickle out of a jar that belonged to her female archenemy, masturbated with it, and then put it back in the jar. I have heard reports of women peeing on other women's toothbrushes. It is subversive and shocking what women can do to each other. They gossip, they spread rumors, they seek to destroy. They will slut-shame. They have no boundaries. They are willing to go down with the ship so long as their object of their ire goes down, too. That is the wonderful instructiveness of the Solomon story in the Bible, when two women claimed motherhood of the same baby. Lost sometimes in the story is the idea that one woman was ready to see a baby cut in half.

The hardest thing to reconcile about the frame of upset and disagreement is that, in so many cases, what's upsetting us has a basis in reality. Yes, there are people who invent all sorts of grievances about their spouses that are untrue. For the rest of us, we're more upset by spouses who leave towels on the bathroom floor, don't do errands when they say they're going to, and make what sounds to us like excuses for their conduct. Or, who change up plans for the holidays without telling in advance.

This relationship thing is not for the faint of heart. We're going to get criticized, and we're going to give criticism. We're going to feel bad, and sometimes other people are going to feel bad on account of us. A thick skin is a good thing in life. Dismantling the frame of upset and disagreement is another good thing. It leads nowhere good, and many places not good. Permit yourself to feel the feelings temporarily, find some meaning in those feelings…and move on.

Kimile Pendleton

THE SIXTH NEGATIVE FRAME:
GUILT AND SHAME

There's not a person alive – well, maybe the worst sociopaths, but I'm not sure I'm ready to classify them as actual "people" – who hasn't been wracked by guilt at one time or another. It's one of the most human of emotions. But what is guilt, exactly? How is that we can go so far astray with it, in two different directions? Either we consistently do things that we feel guilty about, or we feel guilty about things we have no control over. Or both. No matter which path we choose, many of us end up framing our lives with guilt. It is no fun.

When we think about guilt, many of us start with the legal definition, which has to do with a person engaging in conduct that violates a statute of some kind. Doing the act, when there is no legal justification or excuse, makes the person guilty in the eyes of the law. It matters not at all if the person thinks there's perfectly good justification for what they did. This is why a hungry, penniless person can be found guilty of stealing a piece of fruit from a market. Hunger is not a legal justification for the act of theft. Therefore, the person is guilty.

While the legal definition is helpful, what we're more interested in here is psychological guilt – that awful feeling we have all had when we know we haven't lived up to our own expectations for ourselves. Sometimes it is for an act that would make us legally responsible. More often, it is for something that's entirely legal, but we still feel like we haven't done right. Guilt is the feeling of being worthy of blame for having done an act, or failing to do an act, that is in some way an offense from our own perspective. It can be an act that is as psychologically egregious as a man having two families that don't know of each other's existence, or as minor as getting stuck in an unexpected traffic jam and not making it to the start of your kid's soccer game. In both cases, it is perfectly natural to feel guilty, though the degrees of responsibility for the guilty act are very different from each other.

No matter how it manifests, guilt feels terrible. It's not just in our heads, but also in our hearts and souls. Our blood pressure rises, our pores open, our eyebrows narrow, and harrowing thoughts and feelings seem to swim around in us. Sometimes, the guilt goes away in time.

But sometimes, it intensifies. I can think of a client I had in my office who was still ruminating and feeling guilty over an affair she'd had in the second year of her marriage. I felt her pain, and also marveled at the fact that she was still feeling it. This woman was in her mid-seventies, and had racked up forty-eight monogamous years with her husband; she was just about to celebrate her golden anniversary. When I tell you that she was still wracked with guilt for a one-time affair occurrence that had happened when John F. Kennedy had just been inaugurated as president, I am not exaggerating. She lived the vast majority of her married life through the prism of this guilt. Her life was framed by it.

I had another client named Nora, who was in her fifties. Nora was married to Mark. She was a public-school teacher; he was a lawyer. For the first thirty years of their marriage, they had, by general American standards, a reasonably robust sex life—that is, they had sex twice a week. What Nora didn't tell Mark was that she had faked her orgasms during her entire marriage. The only way that she could climax was by masturbation, and she had quit masturbating years before out of guilt. Nora never told Mark about the orgasm-faking thing, that she could reach a climax only by masturbation, or that she had ceased to even masturbate. She told me that she was afraid that he would leave her if she shared these truths with him.

Nora tried everything to work through her sexual issues and alleviate the guilt she felt for not telling Mark what was going on with her. She went to weekend intensives. She swam with dolphins. She fire-walked. She hiked. She dieted. She learned to meditate. She did years of therapy where various therapists told her that it would be in her interest to share with her husband, and she told them that it would be too risky for her.

The status quo was upset when Mark developed serious prostate cancer and needed surgery. The surgery left him impotent, and he thought it might be permanent. Nora found herself guiltier than ever. Mark was lamenting the loss of their sex life. For Nora, it wasn't all that big a loss, but the psychological piece of it was wrecking her. The irony is, once the truth was revealed, a deeper emotional connection between the partners became possible. During the time when sex with penetration was impossible, they were forced to a new reality: sex without penetration. And it worked.

Some education on my part taught them how for the majority of women, orgasms from intercourse alone don't happen. Clitoral stimulation is a must. When the guy can't penetrate and has to connect sexually in a different way, guess what happens in the realm of that stimulation? Yes. You got it. So did Nora.

This story has a happy ending. As Mark's sexual functioning returned – albeit slowly and sporadically – the couple was able to integrate it into a different kind of lovemaking. After decades of sex, they were finally making love. With mutual orgasms, I would add.

I have come to think that guilt is a natural emotion that has a basis both in our attachment to our parents and our own special status as the only creatures on God's green earth with free will and moral memory. When we were infants, our very beings depended on pleasing our caretakers – normally, but not always, our mothers and fathers. A toddler, after all, cannot provide food, shelter, or clothing for himself or herself. Love and acceptance from our caretaker was a clear signal that we would get the safety and sustenance on which our very lives depended. If love and acceptance were forthcoming, food, shelter, and clothing would follow. On the other hand, if we felt rejection and disapproval from our caretaker, it was a reason for our toddler selves to be launched into a panic. It was impossible to have any confidence that food, shelter, and safety were sure things. Therefore, the approval of our caretakers was critical. When our infant, toddler, and childhood behavior didn't merit it, we'd panic. The interior panic of our youth is the basis for the feeling of guilt.

Then there's the spiritual side. The first human story in the bible is the story of Adam, Eve, and the snake in the garden. It is, above all else, a story of guilt: At the behest of the serpent (but where her own free will is, of course, involved), Eve eats from the Tree of the Knowledge of Good and Evil, and shares the fruit of it with Adam. God warned them beforehand that they had complete freedom, but not to eat from the tree, "lest you die."

We all know how the story plays out. Depending on how we read the word "die," God's threat is either carried out or not. Whether this act imbues people with some notion of original sin is likewise a subject for theological debate. What there's no question about at all, and about the only thing in the text that is not subject to debate, is that Adam and Eve felt guilty as all get-out about what they'd done. It was, in fact, a guilt-fest:

Then He asked, "Who told you that you were naked? Did you eat of the tree from which I had forbidden you to eat?"

The man said, "The woman You put at my side – she gave me of the tree, and I ate."

And the Lord God said to the woman, "What is this you have done!"

The woman replied, "The serpent duped me, and I ate."

What a great piece of buck-passing on the part of our biblical forbearers. Adam feels guilty for having disobeyed God, so he tries to pawn off the act onto Eve. Eve feels guilty for her part in this instructional piece of biblical theater, so she tries to pass off the act onto the snake. Those of us who are parents can't help but be reminded of coming home from some event where we've left our old-enough-to-stay-home-alone children in the house to find that the place looking like a federal disaster area. When we question the oldest kid, she or he blames the younger. When we question the younger, she or he blames anyone onto whom blame can be foisted. Both children do this in an effort to remain in our good graces. Nonetheless, everyone involved knows that the children blew it. Including, I might add, the children.

Before we go too much further, it's worth taking a couple of paragraphs to draw a distinction between guilt and shame. These words are often used interchangeably, but they are not the same thing. As I see guilt, it comes out of a place of essential decency. We feel guilty in reaction to something that we have done that will cause disapproval on the part of others if it is discovered, causes self-disapproval in our own hearts whether it is discovered or not, or both. Guilt happens when we've established a code of conduct for ourselves that we can't hold on to.

Shame is something essentially different. Shame is a feeling that we might have about a subject, or ourselves, fundamentally. For example, different world religions – and even denominations within religions – have different notions of mankind essentially being a blank slate, or essentially being sinful. (By the way, this arises out of the same story in Genesis that we discussed just a few minutes ago.) Those who have a core concept of mankind as sinner may well carry around shame because of this fact. That shame becomes an organizing principle for that person in their approach to God.

Shame need not be about our essential relationship with the Almighty, though. It can come from completely human origins. There are whole areas and subject matters that are the subject of shame for many people. Most particularly I see this happen with sex and sexuality, but that's not the only arena. Shame can often arise in self-assessment, and seems to be most powerful in those with insecure or detached childhoods. For example, I've worked with dozens of teens who have come through the foster-care system, or who were adopted. Even when the foster kids land in the most loving of foster homes, or are adopted into truly exemplary families, it is common for these kids to be imbued with an essential shamefulness about themselves. It is as if they are feeling that because their mother did not love them enough to care for them and fight for them, they cannot come to love themselves. Guilt and shame can also coexist. A person who grew up feeling ashamed of him or herself may also feel the same kind of guilt that the rest of us feel. It is like a double-whammy, a double filter through which to try to decipher their lives.

When we feel the familiar spasm of guilt, there are exactly three options before us. First, we can simply live with it in the hopes that it will fade away to some manageable level, or even fade away completely. I had a single male client who traveled for business quite a bit. He understood the guilt he would feel if he were discovered at a massage parlor in the town where he lived – he would feel as if he let down his own community. But the temptation to visit such a parlor was too great for him. So once, on a visit to one of the coasts, he stopped in and paid for a session. He found it perfunctory and somewhat humiliating, and afterward couldn't believe that he'd parted with his hard-earned money for what turned out to be a pretty lousy experience, both actual and moral. Moreover, he felt guilty about it. My counsel was that he not repeat the experience – he'd feel even guiltier the second time – but that he also let time work its magic. He wasn't married. Plenty of us do stupid stuff. In a case like there, where the only victim is the guy himself, turning the guilty experience into a teachable moment is a salutary thing.

The second option is to feel guilty and hide both the feeling of guilt and the thing that makes us feel guilty in the first place. I suppose that a great actor might be able to make his or her life work on the outside while harboring severe feelings of guilt on the inside, but for the rest of us, it's nearly impossible. The truth wants out. The subconscious mind is powerful. When we're holding a secret that makes us feel guilty, the subconscious mind wants that truth to come out, while at the same time, our conscious mind wants us to eject or cover up these almost unbearable feelings of guilt. This is when we see people go to all kinds of lengths to avoid feeling the guilt, like that client of mine who harbored the no-orgasm secret from her husband. We go to therapy. We drink. We meditate. We do drugs. We join support groups and twelve-step groups of all kinds. We do all kinds of things that we think will either provide some sort of balance to the guilt-inducing thing that we have done, or we'll do things that will provide physical and mental sensations that will numb the guilt. What's remarkable is that we have an uncanny ability to keep right on doing the thing that makes us feel guilty even as we're engaging in the activity to assuage or negate those guilty feelings. The great William Shakespeare has a field day with this very human trait, both in his comedies and his tragedies. It makes sense, because it is both risible and sad at the same time.

Then there's the third way that living life through a frame of guilt manifests in our lives. I'm often suspicious when a couple presents themselves in my office with the complaint from one or both of the partners that they just don't feel like they can connect with their husband or wife. She'll say, "We don't have anything to talk about anymore." Or, "We don't have anything in common." Or he'll say, "My wife is so distant all the time, it's like living with a stranger." Or she'll say, "He won't talk to me about anything important. It's always just about the children, or planning the day, or what to have for dinner. Then, he goes and sits in front of the TV."

I had a young couple in my office recently. Call them Nathan and Margot. They're in their 30s, and each had been married before. Each of them brought children into the marriage. The origins of their relationship were controversial. Nathan had met Margot when he was married to someone else; they carried on an affair for two years before Nathan left his wife to marry Margot. Margot similarly left her own marriage to marry Nathan. Obviously, there's a whole lot of psychological burden and guilt coming into this relationship, as well as plenty of wreckage of relationships past.

Nathan proved to be a difficult client. This was a man who specialized in criticism and was darn good at it – small wonder that he worked as an inspector at a manufacturing plant. He habitually criticized everything around him, including me and mine. He criticized everything from the condition of the carpet in my office – too faded, too worn, and too retro – to the lack of a backup security camera in the elevator leading to my floor. His own children were too lazy; Margot's children were too disrespectful. His criticisms were always couched constructively. There was always a suggestion attached for improvement. He reserved much of his criticism for his ex-wife. She was too demanding. She didn't respect his current relationship. She coddled their children. She had been a sexless blob during their marriage and failed to understand that a man like Nathan had sexual needs. In the wake of their marriage, she dated the wrong kind of men.

To my surprise, Margot was actually more generous to the ex-wife than Nathan was. According to Margot, the ex was a reasonably good mother who didn't make untoward demands on anyone. As for her sexlessness, Margot couldn't speak to that directly, but obviously the ex was the past, and Margot was the present. Margot and Nathan described their current sex life together as robust, and Margot wondered what the point was of Nathan's criticizing a woman to whom he was no longer married.

What brought them to my office was Margot's complaint that – you guessed it – Nathan was hypercritical of her. He complained that Margot was boring, that she never wanted to do anything interesting, that she had nothing to say about anything. As a result, Nathan confessed to being on the verge of cheating. He hadn't done it yet, but confessed that he'd come close. The temptation was certainly there, and it was upsetting him.

I asked him what his secret was. He looked at my blankly. I tried it again.

"What's your secret?" I asked, point-blank. "Because what I'm seeing here is the same thing, again and again. You took your first wife, who apparently is not nearly as bad as you make her out to be, and vilify her. Now, you're doing the same thing with your second wife, who most of male America would be happy to come home to on a nightly basis. You're tempted to cheat on her. But what will be the upshot of that? You'll cheat, Margot will toss you out, and you'll have another ex-wife to complain about. Nathan, I wouldn't call that a winning strategy. Would you?"

He looked sheepish. "No."

It took Nathan a while to get to his secret: He had non-normative sexual desires that he felt ashamed and guilty about and could not even confess to Margot. He'd hidden them from the ex, and he was hiding them now. They weren't even all that shocking to me; I'm reasonably unshockable on the sexuality front, so long as laws are not being broken. For Nathan, though, they were humiliating. The longer that he was with a person who made him comfortable, the greater the chance that he might, in a weak moment, confess to his desire to be swaddled in diapers.

It turned out that Margot wasn't so shocked by this, either. Nathan was in no way a baby. It was just what got him off, the same way she had various sexual fantasies of her own that got her off. It was, to her, a big "So what?" She was even okay if Nathan wanted to play around in diapers behind closed doors, though she drew the line at changing that diaper.

Ultimately, Nathan was pulled back from his brink of cheating, blaming his partner, and running away. The truth, for this critical person, set him free.

Here's the thing: Feeling guilty most often involves hiding something. Once the secret is shared, we may feel contrite, or humiliated, or even ashamed, but we don't feel guilty. The person who is feeling guilty will be driven by a fear that they are going to be found out. The most likely situation in which they will be found out is an unguarded moment when their defenses are down and they are in a real connection to another person. That's when unconscious material tends to wend its way to the surface, often in a manner that we're not aware of, even as it happens. So, a person will come to me and say, "So-and-so is acting weird." Or, "So-and-so is so distant." The first thing I think of is that someone may be hiding a secret.

The person hiding a secret or living life stuck in the frame of their guilt may appear to be the opposite of contrite. Rather than becoming distant, they may operate on the theory that a "the best defense is a good offense." These people tend to be extreme. They can get hostile or confrontational easily. They are the people whom we think are impossible to get close to, or who have extraordinarily rigid codes of moral behavior. I am the first to say that exceptions do not prove a rule, but we are all aware of those with rigid moral values in the public world who are engaging privately in the same behavior that is being decried publicly. For them, the best defense of their guilty secret is verbal aggression against the same kind of behavior. It must be a terrible way to live. It is certainly a terrible way to love.

It is so easy for the people who live with a secret-keeper to do what I call "Missing the Withhold." Missing the withhold means overlooking a crucial piece of information that the hypercritical person is not sharing. Whether the person doing the missing is in a real-life relationship or is a counselor like I am, missing the withhold is easy. Early in my career, before I became sensitive to the issue and the possibility, it was something I did from time to time. As I said, one of the recurring defense mechanisms of the person doing the withholding is to go on the offense against us, which activates us and floods us with emotion. When we're flooded, it's easy to be less perceptive. In a way, it is like what a performance magician will do with a misdirect. He or she will want us to watch his left hand, while the trick is being done with his right.

I remember meeting professionally with a group that had come to my office en masse to meet me after having seen me on a media appearance. One of the members was extraordinarily hostile to me. This gentleman came in out of curiosity, he said, but just sat there. He wouldn't even tell me his name. He was totally shut down. I got the oddest feeling that he'd done something terrible in his past. I fussed and fumbled with him, both wanting to draw him out and at the same time avoiding any real probing of what that secret was. Later, I learned that he had mob connections, and was hiding this secret.

I had another client who had told me that before he came to see me, he'd been a professional thief. He specialized in lifting high-tech equipment from offices, and was very good at it. He could spot an expensive computer and knew where he could sell it. One day when he came in, he was acting strangely. I asked him if there was anything he wanted to tell me. He wouldn't talk. I probed. He still wouldn't talk. What had happened was that he'd stolen more computers over the previous several days and assumed that I'd found out. Actually, I was clueless. I missed the withhold, and never saw the client again.

Finally, I remember a couple named Sandee and Bruce, whom I'd seen from time to time. They'd had various financial issues over the course of their ten-year marriage, where Bruce would purchase things without clearing it with Sandee, but those issues were supposedly worked out. Out of the blue, Sandee came to see me because she'd noticed a behavior change in Bruce. He was irritable, he was moody, and there was nothing that she could do to make him happy. She tried and tried, and was getting more depressed by the day. Bruce came in, too, and he was emotionally shut down. Clearly, he was engaged in a withhold from both Sandee and me, but he wouldn't cop to it.

One thing about being a counselor – if people don't talk, you can't listen. I counseled Sandee to be on the lookout for a possible withhold. It took her several months to figure out what that withhold was, but this time I'd diagnosed the situation correctly. Bruce had applied for and received a credit card without any discussion with Sandee. She discovered it by finding the bills in the glove compartment of Bruce's work pickup truck. There was something else in there, too – the bill of sale for a snowmobile that Sandee had no idea had been purchased. Sandee confronted Bruce, who took her to a secret storage unit. In the unit were the snowmobile and other goods he'd bought with the credit card.

Withholds are not always conscious. They can also be done as a way of both testing the partner and distancing in the relationship. It is a way to see if the partner is dialed in, paying attention, and emotionally focused. The withholding partner actually hopes that the other party in the relationship notices that something is wrong. If the withhold is missed, the test is failed.

The best way to avoid living life pinned into a frame of guilt is for us to avoid doing the things that make us feel guilty in the first place. Yet more and more in our interconnected, Facebooked, and Twitterized society, I see people doing things about which they feel guilty as a way of maintaining personal autonomy. I often advise couples not to get too close to each other. Fused relationships are guilt factories, where partners do big and small things about which they feel guilty in order to maintain a degree of separation from their partner; it's a way to avoid psychological smother. I don't recommend it. It's far better not to completely inhabit your partner's heart and soul and have your partner give you some space within the couple than to have a definition of intimacy that provides as much air as a wet blanket. A good fire needs oxygen to breathe.

The next thing that those living through the frame of guilt must consider is that their overall responsibilities don't just run to their own psyches and psychological comfort levels, but also to the comfort levels of others around them. I think back to the older woman who had the affair during the Kennedy administration. Yes, it might cleanse her soul to confess that affair to her husband, but at what cost? Can she predict how he might react? Would it be better to find a way to live with the secret and feel less guilty about it than to confess it and potentially shake the foundation of a long relationship where the partners are now in the third act of their lives? There are times when it is better to let sleeping dogs lie.

But this is a quandary to be teased out; the teasing-out will take some intestinal fortitude, and the solution will be imperfect. To confess the event because it will alleviate your own guilt is not enough, if the confession is going to hurt others. In the words of our Jewish friends, you will be more of a *mensch* if you find a way to keep your big mouth shut. With an affair from forty-eight years ago, it would probably not be difficult to find that way.

Alas, so many of the guilty acts we carry are more significant. A one-time-only affair from forty-eight years ago is simple compared to the situation in the previous chapter of Denise and Gary and Angie and Reed. If I were to reanalyze that situation, I would suspect that there are things that need to be confessed, and things that would be better withheld. Let's face it: When you've got a scene of death and destruction with many victims, triage is the only way to move forward.

The frame of guilt is complicated. There is no one-size-fits-all prescription. In some situations, the adult thing to do is to manage the guilt instead of doing a psychological upchuck on other people that leave us guilt-free but them sullied forever. At worst, guilt is an acid that can corrupt our minds, bodies, and spirits. In the best of all cases, we can use the guilt we righteously feel to become better, more self-actualized, and more intimate, authentic human beings. Guilt is a wonderful motivator. The best motivator of all, of course, is the absence of guilt. If we continually find ourselves doing things that make us guilty, it's time for some real self-reflection and, possibly, professional help.

THE SEVENTH NEGATIVE FRAME:
ADDICTIONS

L og on to any news and entertainment website or app, and it can seem like we are living in the age of addiction. Every celebrity you've ever heard of, and many that you haven't, has been in and out of rehab for drugs, alcohol, or both. Politicians of both parties and professional athletes regularly get caught with their pants down and go away to rehabs of their own. The various "Anonymous" programs, like Alcoholics Anonymous, Narcotics Anonymous, Al-Anon, Sex Addicts Anonymous, Overeaters Anonymous, and Gamblers Anonymous have burgeoning memberships. Talk to people who are regular attendees, and they may speak of their meetings being more like home than the places where they grew up. Celebrity rehab shows capture our interest on television, while battles between rehabilitation professionals in favor of abstinence and those in favor of harm reduction are always good for a point-counterpoint on the morning talk shows.

I want to say something at the outset that may be heresy, but still needs to be said. Addictions can often be killers, chronic and progressive life-shorteners. But not always. They are not, per se, something to be stopped at all costs. On the contrary, addictions can be something that people integrate into their lives. All of us know more than one highly functional alcoholic who gets blitzed when he comes home from work, or on the weekends, but gets himself to work in the mornings without fail and gets his work done well. No one would ever recommend that a person drink as much as the great British wartime leader Winston Churchill or the social critic Christopher Hitchens. If I ever drank as much as those two men did, I wouldn't be able to get out of bed in the morning or write a coherent shopping list, let alone multiple award-winning books or save the western world from Nazism. I know couples whose sexual practices would, by any objective measure, raise big suspicions of sexual addiction, but who have created a moral framework within their relationship that normalizes those practices, and no one suffers for it. It's not something I would do, but it's something they do. They make it work.

At the same time, though, it does no good to underestimate the scourge that addiction can be. The ranks of the homeless, the unemployed, the divorced, the physically and emotionally abusive, and the dysfunctional are populated by addicts. The numbers are staggering. Fifteen percent of the American populace has a drinking problem. The cost of health care for those addicted to tobacco, drugs, or alcohol is $130 billion dollars. Three percent of the population is said to be addicted to sex; around the same number is addicted to gambling. As for addiction to food, all one needs to do is take a walk at the closest mall (or get on the scale or look in the mirror) to get a sense of how many people are overeating, to the detriment of their own health.

And here's the thing: With rare exceptions, every one of those addicts knows what their addiction is doing to them. Every one of them knows what they need to do to make themselves better, and that making themselves better will also make better the people around them who are affected by their behavior. But for one reason or another, the addict either can't stop yet, won't stop yet, or some combination of the two. Sure, there are plenty of addicts who simply can't stop, period. If that person is in a room with alcohol, or they pass a bottle of alcohol, they cannot resist the urge to drink it. If there is crystal meth or cocaine on the table, they will snort it. There must be some sex addicts who cannot say no to any available sex partner, regardless of what she or he looks like, smells like, or what diseases they admit to harboring. It must be a horrible way to live.

Then there are other addicts who seem to be able to stop on a dime, even if, from the outside, the dime is invisible to us, or seems to have been there all the time. I have a friend who was a pack-a-day cigarette smoker. She was well aware of the ill effects of cigarettes; her children would run her cigarettes under water; and yet the woman would not or could not quit. Then, when the woman was in her fifties, her mother died of a heart attack. One day she was fine; three days later, her mother was gone, at the age of seventy-four. That was it. My friend has not smoked a single cigarette since. A person has to live in an isolation chamber to not know that cigarettes are harmful. Somehow, this was the motivation that my friend needed to face reality. The remarkable thing is how it easy it was for her once that motivation was there.

Addiction and the issues surrounding addiction bring a lot of people to my office. Oftentimes, the addiction is normalized in the minds of clients and their families, so the presenting issue will be sexual dysfunction, or a lot of marital fighting, or an inability to control a defiant child. It's only when the family dynamic is explored that it becomes clear how much alcohol one or both parents consume, or how one partner or the other is using their addiction as a way to avoid the pain of living.

I think of my client Michael, who is in his mid-thirties. Michael is married to Rachel, and from the outside, they're a cute couple. They have two children. Michael works construction, and he has since he graduated from college. He's got a knack for it, so he was able to keep working during the economic slowdown. Rachel is dental technician. Together, they're doing just fine financially. What brought them to my office was Rachel's sense that their life was on automatic pilot. He didn't talk to her anymore. He didn't have sex with her anymore. Their conversations were stilted, about the logistics of life and nothing else. As I talked to Michael, I got the sense that I was talking to someone who was saying all the right things but was, at the same time, chafing against his own life. He felt like he needed to be living it, and derived some satisfaction from being able to live it, but in truth, he was fundamentally not cut out for it. He was living a "should" instead of a "want."

Michael did talk to me about his background. He had been raised in Chicago, part of a rigid Christian family. He rebelled by dropping out of high school; he left home to run with a rough crowd. He carried a weapon and became a small-time thief, though he was never arrested. His friends drank, smoke, used drugs; the local strip club was their hangout. In his mid-twenties, he pulled his life together, finished his education, and started working construction. He literally met Rachel in the dentist's chair. She was a model of stability: Good family, good job, good head on her shoulders. He figured she would probably be a good mother, and he was right. She was attracted to Michael's liveliness and edge, and impressed by how he was able to get a handle on a life that easily could have gone in a less productive direction.

Our conversation became more intense as he came to trust me more. He revealed things that he would not reveal to his spouse. As it turned out, Michael never completely let go of his rebel self. As the strictures of conventional living closed in on him, he conducted a secret life that went astray from those strictures. He went to strip clubs with his construction-worker friends, but never told Rachel. He drank more than he should, and did it a lot. At night, after Rachel was asleep, he'd click onto Internet porn and masturbate in secret. When I pointed out the how and why of this secretive existence to him, Michael was at first defensive. Then, he got to talking about the why himself. He wasn't even sure of the why. Then, finally, he chanced talking about it with Rachel, who came to understand Michael's inner rebel and even gave him room to accept himself. I admired her courage, but she said she loved him and it was the least that she could do. Once the underpinnings of the addiction were identified, we could start to do something about it. As a result, Michael's spirits were revived, as were the spirits of their marriage.

I've often said that addicts are the most spiritual people in the world. They feel their feelings intensely even if they cannot name those feelings, they get out of their heads on a regular basis, and they have no difficulty allowing themselves to contemplate the most difficult of issues, which most people just ignore. Why are we here? What are our lives and deaths about? If we can't live forever, then what's the purpose of our existence? Are good and evil real things, or is everything relative? What difference does God make to them? Is there even a God, with all the terrible things that are happening to us and to our planet?

These are the tortuous questions that addicts pose themselves. The questions don't freak them out, but answers that give them no satisfaction do. Or other things can freak them out, the way that a conventional life ripped at my client Michael. When faced with questions that they don't like, answers that they can't abide, or when feeling trapped in a situation from which they think there's no escape, addicts engage in what I'd term a kind of spiritual adultery. If sexual adultery is an inappropriate sexual relationship with a person outside of marriage, and emotional adultery is an inappropriate emotional relationship of the spirit outside of marriage, then addicts are engaged in substance or process adultery. That is, they form a relationship with a process (like eating, sex, or gambling) or a substance (like booze or drugs), and then maintain that relationship come hell or high water, even when the relationship is to their detriment.

At first, the adulterous relationship seems beneficial. Then, it turns self-destructive, almost like a form of slavery. The addict makes promises that he can't keep; he is living under the cloud of the addiction. Then, the addiction operates like a jealous partner, even if the addict can't see how detrimental that partner is to himself. The nightmare of addiction is that even after a moment of lucidity separates the addict from the partner, the siren call can be so powerful that the addict comes crawling back. I wrote of my friend who quit smoking on the news of her mother's death. I am sanguine enough to understand that for every woman like her, there are others who smoke again. Like a partner in an affair, the addiction comes into your space and overrides you. Plus, as a partner in an affair does, the addiction takes up tremendous amount of space, time and focus.

If a person is single, the addiction deflects the person from focusing on other potential romantic relationships, or it can ruin that focus completely. If the addicted person is in a couple, then the addiction latches onto the couple like a tapeworm. The addict is aware of the tapeworm, but the addict's partner isn't, and the tapeworm of addiction sucks the life out of the relationship anyway.

People get addicted to all kinds of things. In our consumer-driven society, with advertising messages coming at us from all fronts, there is a plethora of things that can attract an addictive interest. The old standbys, of course, are alcohol, drugs, food, and sex. But that's not all that there is. All of us know people with closets full of shoes, or a master ranking in a cell-phone game, or even folks who seem to hyperventilate when they are separated from technology. Among our kids and teens, there are many who are addicted to checking their online notifications and social statuses. If there is doubt about the veracity of this, take a cell phone from a teen girl for a weekend and see what happens.

The story of my client Zia may be instructive. She was a lovely young woman in her twenties. Sensitive, compassionate, and thoughtful, she worked at an animal shelter and was known for the way the strays responded to her. However, Zia pulled out her own hair. Trichotillomania is the technical term for this condition. She showed me a picture of herself from age 15 – she had a full head of lush blond hair. When she presented to me, she had a matted, patchy mess on her scalp. Zia knew that this hair-pulling thing was intensely bad for her appearance. As she said to me, "I just can't stop."

Ultimately, we got to the bottom of the addiction. After several sessions, once we built an alliance, Zia recounted how the older brother of a friend had sexually molested her when she was nine years old. During that attack – and it was an attack, I made clear to her – she fixated on the friend's hair as the rape was taking place. In short, the sting of the pain of pulling out her own hair was distracting her from the sting of the psychological pain of what had happened to her. Once we uncovered this, Zia was able to heal, literally and figuratively.

Not every presenting case of addiction is as clear as Zia's. I believe that there are a certain percentage of addicts whose addictions are rooted in repeated childhood Traumas – I use the capital T there deliberately – who cannot stop themselves from drinking, drugging, or whatever. These tend to be people whose lives are a complete disaster. We pity them, with good reason. Their best hope may be to get themselves, or to be put, into an environment where alcohol and other addictive substances are impossible to get. I'm reminded of Denzel Washington's airline-pilot character in the powerful 2012 film *Flight,* who finally got sober only when he went to prison. Not only that, but the character also knew, on some level, that prison was his only hope. People with this kind of addiction are interesting in that they know intuitively how profound their addictions are. Many of them have already cycled in and out of strict religious communities, where the micro-cultural norms are such that they were rarely alone and rarely had access to their addictive substances. Considering that their addictions might well kill them otherwise, those communities are not the worst place in the world for them to be. Faced with a choice of orthodoxy or death, I vote for orthodoxy every time.

With most other people living their lives trapped in the framework of addiction, though, I believe the addiction can be tackled once we unpack the reasons that the solution of addiction worked psychologically for the person on a short-term basis. It's easy to get reductionist here; people's psychologies are complicated. Yet I feel confident in saying that when we understand the problem to which the imperfect solution of addiction provides an answer, there's every chance the addiction will wither. For some people, there is an unwanted condition in their lives, like anxiety, shyness, or frustrations. For others, the addiction is a third answer to the twin horns of an impassible quandary. For others, it's a death wish.

Addictions wreck lives. They wreck the lives of the addict, and they wreck the lives of people around the addicts. If an addiction is your framework for living, it's not functional in the long run. You know it, too. All that's left is to change it.

LEVELS OF HUMAN EXISTENCE #1:
SEX

Life has joys, and life has sorrows. Triumphs, and disasters. Things that are easy, and things that are hard. Life, and death. And then there's sex.

Sex is the thing that sets your couple relationship apart from all others. The truth is that a person can have awesomely close connections with all manner of people. Most of us have at least one friend whom we count as a soul friend, and some of us are fortunate to have a coterie of people as emotional intimates. Some folks are even part of a network of friends who routinely bares their souls to one another. A person can go to a movie with a friend, have dinner with a friend, and talk for hours in a park or over a cold drink with a friend. But for most of us – and no disrespect to those who've opted for another way, whatever works for you and is authentic – sex is something that is confined by the boundaries with our intimate partner. And small wonder: in most cases, affairs (and by that I mean secret sexual relationships, not sex with others when primary partners are aware and give the okay) are devastating. Many marriages recover from an affair, but many do not. As a general rule, if you'd like to remain married to your sexual partner, it's probably better not to test the waters to determine if yours is one of those that can come back.

Sex is a recurrent issue in the lives of committed couples – well, most committed couples, anyway. There are the storied and treasured few who seem to be able to play the lifelong sexual toccata and fugue like an accomplished duo on harpsichord and violin, the music rising and falling in intensity as the score calls for it, always part of a coherent and sweet-sounding whole. For the rest of us, it isn't such an effortless thing. And the thing is, sex often starts out, if not in fireworks, at least okay. There's the excitement of newness, and the rush of having a ready partner to whom we're attracted. (If we're marrying someone to whom we're not sexually attracted, there had better be a serious discussion before the marriage happens, and the partner better not be expecting a lot of sexual participation from us. Otherwise, prepare for the train wreck.)

When the discussion does take place, it can bring the couple together in a marvelous way. I worked with a couple in their fifties who had been married for thirty years. Like all marriages, it had its ups and downs, but sex was one of the areas where the marriage flourished. These two people, Georgia and Walter, had a great sex life. Thirty years later, they were still having passionate sex several times a week. They made sex a priority. They may not have had the biggest house on the block or the newest car, but sexually, they were very content.

Then, life happened. Georgia was diagnosed with serious ovarian cancer that required major surgery. Sex was going to be out of the question for the foreseeable future. Walter and Georgia talked about the implications of this, and Georgia was quite willing to negotiate some arrangement for Walter. It was an act of supreme courage and love. I wondered whether I would be capable of doing the same, were I in the same position. Even so, Walter refused. He said that they'd had a great sex life for so long that he wanted to go through the deprivation of sex with Georgia. Basically, he said that if she was going to starve, he was going to starve with her. Georgia was sacrificing sex against her will; Walter was going to sacrifice sex out of solidarity with the wife he loved. When they told me about this decision, which they made after several sessions with me, I cried a little bit. There was a nobility and stoicism to it that was deeply touching.

On the other end of the sexual spectrum from Georgia and Walter, we find couples for whom sex is not a big deal. Every couple comes together for its own reasons. There are couples for whom physical attraction is paramount. There are others where the partners are fine to live with someone to whom they are not really attracted, because attraction is, in their estimation, highly overrated. These couples may find the most important common ground of their marriage in their work. They may find it in their religious observance or practices. They may find it in children. Paradoxically, they may end up with enormous families, through sex strictly for procreation, and adoption. I have come to believe that just as there is a continuum for everything in life, from low to high, from little to great, there is a continuum for sexual desire. The key is for couples to match up in their desires the same way they match up in other things.

Part of the reason that sex becomes such a point of relationship contention is that men and women have different biological configurations.

I'm fond of telling women that they should recall, or try to imagine (if they've not had a child), the experience of breast-feeding a baby. I'm not referring to the warm, gushy feeling that comes from having an infant at the nipple and the kind of primal connection between mother and baby that the experience triggers. That is an amazing and lovely experience, but it's not the one I'm talking about. What I'm talking about is that feeling that a woman gets when her breasts are bursting with milk, and there's no baby to take sustenance. Yeah. That one. Ouch. It doesn't exactly hurt, but it's incredibly uncomfortable. As far as I know, there is only one way to make it better.

Now, journey southward in the male anatomy, and you'll get what I mean about men being configured differently. Men have their own version of biological build-up and need for release. The more virile they are – the more they have the kind of manly characteristics that women are attracted to as a matter of biology and wiring of their own – the more this build-up of semen is going to happen. Just as with women, they need release. As far as I know, there's only one way, as with the nursing mother, to make the uncomfortable feeling all better. The difference is that the nursing mother has no problem talking about her need to nurse. In fact, it's a badge of honor, written about in popular magazines and talked about on Oprah's show. Now, imagine a guy talking in polite company about his need for sex, or writing about it in the *Los Angeles Times*. I can imagine it well. He'd be shunned. Women would think he's uncouth, men would think he's talking about something that shouldn't be spoken about, and everyone would think he's a boor. The fact is, men are largely alone when it comes to acceptance of their most basic thoughts and desires for sex. Not only that, but they also don't really want to talk about it. They don't need to communicate about it. What they need, at the most basic level, is to *do it*.

Where things get particularly tricky when it comes to doing it is in the long-term relationship. By long-term relationship, I'm talking about relationships that have moved into their third year or beyond. As usual, some of the problem is biological and psychological. Sexologists have long pointed to a phenomenon called the "Coolidge" effect, named after the one-term president from the 1920s, Calvin Coolidge. Reportedly, Coolidge and his wife were touring a chicken farm. Mrs. Coolidge took a look at the chicken area and saw many females, but just one rooster. She asked the man in charge if that single rooster was sufficient to keep the hens satisfied.

"Yes, for sure," said the supervisor. "That rooster works hard."

"Really?" Mrs. Coolidge asked. "He can take care of all of them?"

"Absolutely. Dozens of times every day," the supervisor reported.

Mrs. Coolidge laughed. "That's fascinating. Maybe you should share that information with the president."

When President Coolidge was told about this encounter between his wife and the supervisor, he had a question of his own. "That rooster does the same hen every time?"

"Oh no! Not at all, Mr. President," the chicken supervisor explained. "That yard is full of hundreds of chickens."

The president nodded sagely. "Tell that to my wife."

In long-term relationships, there's just one rooster and one hen. It's not impossible to maintain a solid sexual alliance, but it is not the same thing as when the rooster meets the hen for the first time. When that alliance begins to falter, both partners can feel starved for the kind of sex they want. We all know that starvation is a negative. We can endure it for a time, but after too long, it becomes debilitating. Ultimately, it will kill us. When we get starved for sex, and for the feelings that can and should be associated with sex, it doesn't stop our hearts or shut down our kidneys like when we're starved for food and water. Instead, it wrecks our spirit. In many cases, people who feel sexually starved begin to look for other "food." We all know what that means. It can be an affair, pornography, secret masturbation, an online emotional connection or office romance, visits to prostitutes and sex workers...the list goes on. In general – and again, I emphasize the general nature of this, since male and female psychologies can and do meet in the middle – it tends to be the guy who starts looking elsewhere.

I am often surprised by the range of people who tell me that they've gone outside their marriages for sex. It is unpredictable. There are some cases where it is more likely than others. People who, for some reason, cannot own their core sexual identity within their marriages may well find themselves satisfying themselves outside. Some of the examples of this are people who are living "straight" while actually being gay, and those with particular fetishes too embarrassing to bring into the marriage, and the like. There are people with particularly conventional public appearances that are assumed to help cover less-conventional sexual urges. We all know the cases of the televangelists who have been caught in sexual dalliances, both heterosexual and homosexual. Other leaders of society, whether political, social, or religious, can seem equally prone. I remember a Mormon bishop who lived a straight life, but was actually gay. He lived in an essentially sexless marriage for many years, and had one child. Havoc was wreaked when he gave everything up to live a life true to his sexuality. He blew up his family, his church, and his community. There was devastation in his life, and devastation in his wake. If only his world were one where he could feel comfortable to live authentically.

I had a client named Tara, a woman in her thirties in a marriage of ten years. She worked as a school administrator; her husband was a surveyor who spent much time on the road away from home. To make some secret extra money, Tara – a truly beautiful woman – found a gig stripping at a bar many miles from home. She did it initially for the money, but came to find the work and the power intensely exciting. She was propositioned by a couple of her customers and accepted their invitations. She didn't work as an escort, exactly. Her only clients were these two men. Yet the combination of the money and the power made it almost impossible to stop. The story did not end conventionally. She and her husband divorced, because she did not want to stop.

As couples build and grow and life circumstances change, the couple will automatically need to renegotiate any number of things that seemed clear during the initial romance but are not so clear two, three, or ten years later: Where to live. Where to pray. Where to work. Who's going to be in charge of what. It is almost a given that the way the couple has arranged their life at the start of the relationship is not the way the couple will be, precisely, after the relationship has endured for several years, or even decades. Yet as a culture, we seem far more willing to have an intimate discussion about renegotiating every other possible subject than we are to have a discussion about renegotiating sex.

It's not a comfortable conversation. These are intense and intimate talks that cut to the core of your beliefs and assumptions about the world, yourself, your upbringing, and your plans for the future. These are not conversations for sissies. But long-term relationships are not for sissies, either. The thing is, if the conversations are not had, the renegotiation is going to happen anyway. There will be new patterns of behavior that emerge for both you and your partner; the difference is that those patterns will be implicit instead of explicit, and their corrosive effect on your relationship will be more powerful. What I'm saying is that renegotiation is inevitable. It can be implicit or explicit, discussed or not discussed at all, by design or by accident, out in the open or in secret. For the sake of your relationship and all the wonderful things that come along with it, the better choice is for an explicit, discussed, designed, open review and revision of how you are sexually with each other. The alternative is risky.

It is always dangerous to talk in generalities about sex and sexual desire, but the statistics indicate that male sexual desire endures longer and sustains more intensely than that of women. By the time partners have been in a long-term marriage, it is not unlikely that it is going to be the man's desire that is still there and the woman's that has waned. It's not always that way, however. What is inevitable is that there's going to be a change from how things were when the couple came together. The keeping of sexual secrets through the marriage can make the renegotiation of sex at a later date a trickier enterprise.

If the conversation can be had and survived – and you will survive it, as long as your starting place and goal is the strengthening of your couple bond, and not the wrecking of it – your relationship will be stronger for it. This is the kind of conversation that is tailor-made for a marriage. It is a conversation that can take place only between intimate partners. It's a conversation that is private and should stay private. The goal of the conversation is both noble and necessary. When the conversation is over, you will feel both relieved and strengthened. I liken it to the sex talk that we all have – or at least, should have – with our teens before they get sexually active. Sexual activity will come for them. Some of them will be abstinent; others will be sexually active. Even the absence of sex is reflective of a stance on sex. That sex talk with your teen is not a comfortable conversation for many of us. It can be downright nerve-racking. Yet if the conversation – better, a series of talks – does not happen, the sexual activity will take place anyway. If abstinence on the part of your teen is the goal, then it needs to be talked about. If responsible sexual contact is the goal, it needs to be talked about. It's the same thing with the renegotiation of sexuality in longstanding couples. It needs to be talked about, since it's going to take place anyway. It is either going to take place before the behavior changes, or afterward. Before the behavior changes is a lot less emotionally charged. It is a bit like the difference between deciding to discuss what color to repaint a room before the fresh paint goes up on the wall, and afterward. Only no one gets divorced because of repainting.

One of the keys is to overcome the various things that can get in the way of the conversation. There are strong societal reasons for feeling uncomfortable about discussing the renegotiation. First, we're a youth-worshipping society. We don't like to acknowledge in any way that we are not as young as we once were, and that the sexuality of a long-term relationship is different from the flash-bang of a new couple. There is obvious romance in the newness. Remember Coolidge's chickens. Those feelings of romance are fairly consistent across couples and across cultures where partners couple for love. How things shake out in the couple for the long term is a different matter. Each couple is different.

We don't like to acknowledge that older people can have vibrant sex lives, or should have vibrant sex lives. The trope of teenagers wincing at the idea of their parents "doing it" is a trope for a reason. It is the same trope with which we all grew up. When we become our parents' age, it is hard to acknowledge that sexuality is something that we care about. The conventional wisdom is that it should fade away like the leaves in the fall. The conventional wisdom is not very wise on this issue. Sexuality changes, but it does not fade way.

Health is also an issue. It changes, it is unpredictable, and no matter how much we try to control our own destinies, genetics play a big role in our physicality. When one isn't feeling great, it's hard to feel great about sex. At the same time, modern medicine has made it possible for people to live with chronic diseases for decades. In the past, illness and infection were killers. Now, they are something to be controlled. Truth be told, our grandparents and their ancestors didn't have to think much about what it would be like to factor sex into a relationship where chronic illness played a role, because those relationships were time-limited. Now, it's familiar territory, even if we don't exactly know what the map of that territory should look like. In the past, issues would not need to be renegotiated because the same factors that led to the need for renegotiation were factors that ended marriage because of death and disease. Fortunately, that is no longer the case.

The frames that we apply to our lives also come into play in the arena of sex. Those who live life caught in the frame of victimhood have stumbled into a goldmine if their sex life in the couple is not what they dreamed. There are so many things that can victimize these folks. They're victimized by their partners (who are either frigid, withholding, cheating, or maniacal) and they're also victimized by the changes in their life circumstances that have caused their sex life to deteriorate or even disintegrate. It can be aging, illness, children, job pressures, relocation, menopause, hormones…there is always something to be victimized by. The paradox is that the worse the person has it, the better his or her story. The better the story, the more the sympathy. The more the sympathy, the more reason to stand by the story and not change it. Plus, to be victimized by sex, by a cheating husband or wife, is a completely socially acceptable victimization. (As a rule, this tends to be a female thing. For men to complain of sexual victimhood is socially unacceptable and humiliating. If you want confirmation, when their partners cheat, men are called cuckolds. Yet women are victimized by their cheating husbands).

The same holds true for the other framing devices for our lives. Those living life stuck in the frame of the reenactment of fear and trauma will experience the feelings of their earlier traumas in the disruption and disconnection of their current sexual difficulties. Those previous traumas will underscore their current belief system.

Those whose frame is quandaries? Well, there's no place like the conjugal bed to find yourself in a quandary – or maybe in more than one quandary. There are feelings that if you want to do a certain thing, you will be shamed or belittled. Or that if the practice that turns you on is legal but socially laughable – let's say you like feet as much as you like lips – you will be shamed or belittled. Or that if someone ever found out that you liked your partner to dress in a certain way, or reenact a certain scenario, or that you wanted to open your marriage to the possibility of other sexual partners, you will be shamed or belittled. Those are real quandaries.

If you're coming to sexuality in a long-term relationship under the heel of an oppressor, then you've also got a massive challenge on your hands. It is hard to find your own way in your sexuality if you feel manipulated, or if you are being manipulated without knowing it. In fact, it's hard to find your true self.

Your true sexual self may well change over the course of your relationship. This chapter argues that it is nearly inevitable that it will. How you and your partner do the renegotiation of sex as those changes happen is entirely up to you. The beauty of the bedroom door is that no one has to know what is on the other side. You need not share it with anyone if you don't want to share it. Clients ask me about real or perceived kinks, real or perceived issues with open marriages, real or perceived issues with their sexualities. My answer is almost always underpinned by the notion that marital sexuality is a marital matter. So is sex in a committed relationship. This is not to say that society has no interest. It does, and there are laws on the books to back it up. But if what one is doing runs afoul of no laws – if it is not bestiality or pedophilia that is the issue, but simply feelings and change – then it's between you and your partner to negotiate and renegotiate. You will be better, closer, more intimate, and more connected partners as a result.

LEVELS OF HUMAN EXISTENCE #2:
FOOD AND YOU

The great humanistic psychologist Abraham Maslow wrote about something he called the hierarchy of human needs. In its simplest terms, Maslow built a pyramid. At the bottom of the pyramid, at the foundation just aboveground, were the principal things we all need to survive. They're not fancy, they're not complicated, and they're not psychological. They're physical. Without the satisfaction of these basic (in the strictest sense) needs, humans not only can't flourish, but they also can't even survive and reproduce. They're doomed.

From that base, once those needs are taken care of, we move up the pyramid through our safety needs, our love and belonging needs, and our esteem needs, until we reach a level of needs that Maslow calls "self-actualizing" and that I call "living in harmony." More on "self-actualization" and living in harmony later. For now, we're interested in the more primitive stuff, which is easy to overlook or take for granted in our high-tech world, but is crucial.

At the most foundational level of needs is those physiological needs. Maslow ticks off such basic human requirements as breathing. Water. Sleep. Health. Bodily functions, like excretion and breathing. Sex. Food. He's got an important point. When any one of these things is disrupted for us, life itself is threatened. Without water, we die. Without sleep, we struggle and eventually die. Without health, life can be a living hell. Without bodily function, we die. Without sex…well, we talked about sex in the previous chapter. If there's actually no sex, the species will die. If there's so little sex that resentment simmers and boils in the relationship, sometimes it feels like death would be a pleasant alternative.

Then there's food. It's not an accident that I am placing a discussion of sex and a discussion of food back to back. They are both big issues, particularly here in America. And they have far more in common than many people would imagine at first blush. In a society where we want to intellectualize and compartmentalize everything, to analyze, categorize, and discuss everything to death and then some, sex and food stand out as non-intellectual incorrigibles. They are basic Maslovian (things pertaining to Maslow's theories are called Maslovian, not Maslowian – it's easier to pronounce) primal needs that don't have a whole lot to do with reading, writing, and arithmetic. The instincts that trigger both sex and eating are physical and primal. The satisfaction that we get from a positive sexual experience and a satisfying nourishing meal are, in many ways, the same. The similar reactions are as much in our bodies as in our minds. Actually, more so: There are changes in heart rate, breathing rate, hormone balance, and brain chemistry that come from good sex. There are changes in heart rate, breathing rate, hormone balance, and brain chemistry that come from good food. These changes take place regardless of what we are thinking we would like them to be. Just try to *think* your body into not responding when someone you desire kisses you, or to *think* your body into not taking nutrition and pleasure from a well-cooked, well-presented, well-balanced meal. It's well-nigh impossible. These are two of the arenas where what we think doesn't matter much when we're in the middle of the experience. No wonder Maslow identified them as basic needs. Both are physical. In a poetic sense, with both sex and nourishment, you are taking something into your body and making it a part of you temporarily, and then permanently.

Both food and sex hearken back to a purer, simpler time in our lives. Before any of us reached adolescence, the greatest bodily pleasure that we could experience, on a regular basis, came from food. This is not to say that kids don't masturbate. They do. But infants at the breast of their mother, or at the bottle, get a pure and life-affirming feeling from the flow of milk into their systems. It is not simply a matter of nourishment, but also a matter of connection between parent and child. It is a sensual thing that we associate not just with the food, but also with sensuality. No wonder, then, that as the Internet has grown, the two areas of greatest growth have been in pornography and food blogging and writing. If a person has a pulse, they don't have to be informed about the pornification of the Internet. But the "foodification" is almost as significant. Food bloggers are online superstars. Recipe sites are ridiculously popular. Restaurants and food stores are relentlessly reviewed and dissected at Yelp and other reviews sites. The public eats it up – pun very much intended.

However, there is a flip side to our primal obsession with food. America is a big country. I am not just referring to the distance from Hawaii to

Maine. What I'm targeting is our waistlines. More than any other country on Earth, we're fat. Scientists and social scientists have tried to blame our expanding pant and dress sizes on everything from the ready availability of fast food to the allure of the flat-screen television. But the fact remains that fast food is for sale in every civilized country in the world, and costs someone in Paris or Tel Aviv no more than it does someone in Denver or Duluth. Similarly, everybody has access to television, and the Internet has made the world's programming available to everyone. Judging from our waistlines, there's something special going on here in these United States, and I would venture to say that it has to do with our individual psychologies. Once we've got those psychological issues diagnosed, we can look at how to fix them.

Before we look inward, though, it is worth looking outward. Sweet stuff and television have been around for a long time. It is only in the past couple of decades that we've seen the explosion of obesity that has even gotten the attention of the White House. First lady Michelle Obama made it a priority to spearhead a nonpartisan drive against childhood obesity, on the theory that if we can stop children from overeating and under-exercising, there is a better chance that those same children, once they become adults, will be healthier people as well.

It's not an easy fight. The enemy has grown more cunning. A feature in the *New York Times Magazine*, "The Extraordinary Science of Addictive Junk Food," by Michael Moss, details the amazing, sobering, and somewhat frightening efforts by food companies like Pillsbury and Oscar-Mayer to fine-tune the taste and other characteristics of everything from Doritos to Lunchables in order to keep us coming back for more. It's worth tracking down that article, because the detailed reporting is so compelling. Suffice it to say that everything in a Dorito, from the taste balance to the size of the chips to the color and texture of the packaging, is designed to convert a one-time purchaser into a lifelong purchaser. The Lunchable that we so blithely pack for our kids to take to camp or elementary school is the object of similar study and scientific development.

The social critics Marnia Robinson and Gary Wilson think there's a reason for this, and posit that it's the same reason that more people are finding an unnatural attraction to pornography than ever before. Robinson and Wilson refer to food and sex as "natural reinforcers." That means that sex and food light up the pleasure centers of our brains automatically, and are natural biological needs. A gambler needs the rush of gambling, but gambling is not necessary to get through life and to reproduce. Same thing with a heroin addict. Sex and food, though, are different. They're necessary. That makes them all the more powerful.

Robinson and Wilson make the argument that highly refined, super-stimulating food – food that's full of artificial flavors that go beyond any found in nature, with unnaturally high concentrations of fat, and sugar that has been refined in a way that our cavemen ancestors could never dream – has an effect on the brain akin to the rush of gambling for the gambling addict or alcohol for the alcohol. Not all food does this, just the super-stimulating ones. They make the same argument about high-speed Internet pornography, arguing that it can and does affect the pleasure centers of the brain in a way that our parents' and grandparents' pornographic photographs and books never could. The writers suggest that when we eat normally and healthfully, there is a natural balance between the good feelings of pleasure that come with eating well and the feeling of being satiated. That is, after the second grilled backyard hamburger, no matter how good it is, we probably don't want to eat more. We're full. The idea of a third, fourth, or fifth burger, or even a third, fourth or fifth veggie burger, is actually off-putting. Who among us has not heard, or said with sincerity, "It's delicious, but I can't eat another thing. Thank you so much for the spectacular meal!"

Not so with super-stimulating foods like processed meats, Hostess whatevers, highly salted chips, and the like. Here, the balance gets tipped in favor of super-stimulation. The hyped-up flavors – remember, the manufacturers have spent millions of dollars getting those foods to the optimal taste and texture for maximum consumption – override the normal boundary of feeling full. It's not all that different from how it was with our cavemen ancestors, who didn't know where their next meal was coming from. If they managed to kill a mastodon, they ate and ate until they couldn't eat anymore, even if they were full. Survival required it. These days, we don't have to eat like that. We know where the next meal is coming from, most of the time. But the super-stimulating and processed foods make the override of the satiation stop-eating trigger inevitable.

Small wonder, then, that so many of us are fighting the battle of the bulge. When we send our kids to school with Lunchables because all their friends are bringing Lunchables and we know they'll actually eat it, we're setting a pattern for years to come. Kids gravitate to the high-calorie, low-nutrition versions of these foods. When Oscar Mayer tried to bring out a healthier version of Lunchables, they sold poorly.

As Robinson writes in a blog for *Huffington Post*, the food is there in unlimited varieties and limitless quantities. Like sex, it's at the bottom of the Maslovian hierarchy. We need it to survive. Most of us have no idea why we're eating as much of it as we are. So is it any surprise that the majority of Americans are overweight, and a third of us are clinically obese? Not to me it isn't. I'm not personally immune to the lure of overeating – not hardly, as my family can tell you. It's been a lifelong struggle for me as it has been for many.

I've refrained from discussing here much of my own life experience, but in the arena of weight and diet, that experience can be instructive in many ways. As a girl, I began to overeat in response to a specific and identifiable trauma, and overeating has been my own particular bugaboo ever since. It waxes and wanes as an issue in my life, normally in response to how much stress I am feeling. When it comes to food, there are two possible dietary responses. There are people who can't stomach food, and those who can stomach too much of it. We all know people who fit into both categories. I fit into that second one.

I grew in one of those safe communities where children can walk to school without parental supervision. My family's house was on one side of a small park, and my elementary school was on the other side. It may be hard for many of today's parents to understand, but it was normal for parents to send their kids off to school in the morning with a kiss and a "Have a great day."

I look at pictures of myself from kindergarten, first grade, and second grade, and I see a normal-weight, happy girl. All that changed in third grade, after this significant trauma. Even now, I can picture it. What happened was that I was walking to school with some friends. It was at the end of my kindergarten year. I was an experienced walk-to-schooler at that point. There was a group of us, and one of the boys in the group was being mean to me. Intelligently, I hung back from the group as we crossed Veterans Park, letting some significant physical space get between the boy and me.

That's when I was grabbed by a man I didn't know. I wasn't taken for very long – less than a day. I was not physically assaulted, nor sexually abused. The chances of what happened to me happening to others is miniscule, because the odds of a child being abducted by a stranger are less than the chances of a person dying in a lightning strike. I must say that if I had an elementary school child, and was in the same kind of community again, I would permit that child to walk to school on his or her own. That's how unlikely what happened to me was. Yet it did happen. The guy who grabbed me and took me under his coat had ice-blue eyes and gray hair in a butch cut. He was, in my estimation a very, very big man. He wore military clothes and was most likely a veteran.

Strangely, he kept me next to him in the park and did not try to transport me anywhere until the end of my time with him. In retrospect, I had it easy. He just warned me not to cry out. In those days, schools did not call parents when a child was absent. My half-day kindergarten teacher just assumed that I was sick, and my mom assumed that I was in school. The friends I was walking with were in a different class, so they didn't even realize I hadn't come to school.

After what seemed like an eternity, I was rescued in the most banal of ways. My friend Nancy's mom was picking her up. The man had me in the park with his hand over my mouth and was carrying me toward the parking lot. I knew if I left with him I would never go home. I don't know how I knew that but I did. I was frozen, terrified and completely out of my body. I was also afraid of getting into trouble with my mom for being late. Odd, I know, but I was equally afraid of disappointing my mother. No matter what, I just knew I had to go home,

As we moved toward the parking lot, he had me inside his bulky winter coat. His hand covered my mouth. I did the smartest thing of my life to that point. I bit him. He yelped, but let go of me. I wisely ran away. He chased me. My friend Nancy's mother saw me, rolled down her window and heard me screaming, "Big man! Big man!" She pulled over, I opened her car door, jumped in, and got hysterical. I could hardly get the words out. I was crying and saying "Big man, Big man!" over and over.

Nancy's mother drove off. By the time she deduced what had happened, we were blocks from the park. She brought me home and talked to my mom, who called the local police. They launched an investigation, but couldn't find the guy. Apparently, that was the end of it.

Except for me, it wasn't the end of it. Not in a subconscious way, anyway. My family didn't talk about the incident because they didn't want to upset me. I didn't want to talk, period. In the months afterward, I began to stutter. I'm sure that sounds impossible to those who know me now, but it's true. I feared big men with blue eyes, because the man who had grabbed me was big and had blue eyes. I didn't like to be touched, or to be in any situation that was out of my control. I got these mysterious stomachaches that had no medical explanation. The psychological explanation was, of course, anxiety, but people were not so psychologically sophisticated back then, or as fast to get children into therapy following an identifiable trauma.

The stomachaches felt better when I ate. I had a grandmother who was a brilliant cook and baker. I found that eating sugary treats was especially anxiety-relieving. Were I older, maybe I would have turned to marijuana or other drugs. But I wasn't older. I was a kid, and my grandmother's baking was downright spectacular. I became a connoisseur of cake and cookies, and a duchess of doughnuts. The higher the carbohydrate content, the less my stomach ached and the better I felt.

It wasn't until I was older, and realized with cognitive therapy that a shift in what I consumed meant that I'd be a healthier person, that I was able to bring the weight thing under control. And even now when stress rises, food issues its alluring call.

The thing is, to be alive is to feel stress and anxiety. In a way, those two things signal that we care. Surely there are some people who can live placidly and die at ninety-five with unlined faces, but I don't know any of them. To be alive and to be a conscious person is to be, in some way, anxious. After all, we're living on this knife's edge: Our world is finite. After we're gone, it will go on in its merry way without us. If that fact doesn't make you feel insignificant and anxious, you're a blessed outlier. For most of us, the issue is not whether to be anxious or not, but what we do with this anxiety. A lot of people eat. Food becomes the solution to the problem. Alcohol becomes a solution to the problem. Xanax becomes a solution to the problem. For teens, self-injury can be the solution to the problem. We hold anxiety both in our minds and in our bodies, so it's no wonder that many of us seek a physical solution for the bad feelings.

What do I do now with the anxiety of life? I don't take Xanax or other medications. Some natural herbs are good; GABA and L-theanine from green tea are good, too. I try to accept the anxiety I feel and not let it overwhelm me unless it has to. That is, if I – God forbid! – just got the news that I have been diagnosed with terminal cancer, there's no big issue with eating a pint of Haagen-Dazs. But when the source of the anxiety is manageable, I try to manage it by being conscious of both mind and body. The key is to find a way to self-soothe that is not self-destructive. We need to calm ourselves down, meditate, and talk through the issues that are making us anxious. Even with conscious eating, though, it's incredibly revelatory to get a sense of how the deck is stacked against us, as Robinson and Wilson so ably point out.

Finally, though, it is through our mouths that this food must travel. And the fact remains that not all of us are overeating and overweight, even with the array of temptations that awaits us wherever we may shop. This is the difference between those who are gaining weight and those who maintain their weight where they want it to be.

There are many facets to any individual's relationship with food. Many are rooted in childhood and adolescence. We talked before of the infant at the breast of the mother or the bottle held by the caretaker. The nature of that relationship can unconsciously shape a person's relationship with food. If, for the child, feeding time is the calmest time of his or her day, then food will become associated with comfort and safety. Feeding will actually trigger those positive psychological feelings. In a world as turbulent as our own, with so many uncertainties and things not under our control, to find a place of comfort and safety can be extraordinarily meaningful. It is, in some ways, like a ritual: Engage in the ritual, and get the feeling. For example, in the adult world, when we think about the ways that we celebrate our holidays and festivals, food is almost always a part of the celebration. Thanksgiving, Christmas, weddings, wakes, and more are marked by meals. For those occasions, we don't get together to eat just because we happen to be hungry. If it were just that, we could order in pizza for Christmas dinner and serve Doritos Locos Tacos at a wedding feast. However, we ritually go all-out for these meals. We cook from scratch. We gather around the table to partake of turkey that has been in the oven for hours. When we think back to Thanksgivings past, we might have some fleeting memory of a parade watched on television, but it's the Thanksgiving dinners that stand out. Those dinners occupy a place of comfort and safety in our minds.

Food becomes the expression of the emotional component of eating. It becomes part of our very character. I've often observed that people who take on much responsibility for the welfare of others, as many mothers do, are large and in charge – literally as well as figuratively. Those who are emotionally lightweight can afford to be lightweight. Those whose daily existence requires them to serve the basic Maslovian needs of others tend to be well-fortified for the task. Our vision of the typical foster mom to multiple kids, for example, is not of a skinny woman. There are exceptions to every rule, but I suspect that many would agree with me when I suggest that they tend to be bigger. Then, of course, their sheer bigness becomes something else to try to take care of and manage.

People can also have an almost sadomasochistic emotional relationship with food. There are those who hate food. I'm not talking about the anorexics whose complex psychologies are beyond the scope of this book. I'm referring to the women – and, yes, most of them are women – who try to attain power over food through denial of it to their selves. In that same way, in that self-denial, they are attaining some version of power over themselves. It's not a pretty term, but I think of them as "Skinny Bitches." We've all run into them at one time or another – or, more likely, they run into us, flaunting their boyish bodies, implanted breasts, and green-centered meals. Never do they cop to consuming more than a thousand calories a day. These are the women who take pleasure in the self-denial of bodily pleasure like food and sex, and use their bodies as a sort of human Venus flytrap. That is, the body lures men in, and then kills them off because the satisfaction is in the luring instead of the relationship. For these women, there is no way any man could provide the same kind of pleasure that she gains from her self-denial. They who take pleasure in the feelings of deprivation that come with dieting see their own ability to tolerate the discomfort as a sign that they are superior to the rest of us mere mortals. There is self-affirmation every time that they glance in the mirror. Never mind that they are depriving themselves the joy of a great meal with friends, a Christmas dinner with family, or even the steadiness that comes with moderation and a sound emotional relationship with food. None of those things matter. If they do matter at all, they don't matter enough.

A woman named Darla came into my practice. She was in her forties, and she first saw me because her boyfriend, Tony, had caught her cheating. To his credit, he did not want to end the relationship without some serious inner work. Rarely have I encountered such a paradoxical woman as Darla. She was brilliant, incisive, analytical, and almost ruthlessly practical. At the same time, the way that she applied her brilliance, incisiveness, powers of analysis, and groundedness left me shaking my head. Her entire existence had to do with the exertion of power over men, and attainment of power over men. She tended to pursue this power both for the perks it brought her, and the rush of the experience itself. Women can be incredibly headstrong, and that character trait can be a gift. But never had I seen anyone being headstrong in the direction that Darla presented herself.

Darla had an unusual upbringing that colored her approach to life. Her dad was a B-list famous person. He managed a very famous A-list contemporary music artist. Her father was the best kind of a micromanager for his client. He was obsessed with appearances and seemed to have a preternatural skill at managing his client's image. As a result, this client prospered for years longer than most pop artists do. Darla grew up with the notion that it's important to look good, because what someone thinks about a person's image can affect his or her entire life. She got this lesson from watching her father, but took it to an extreme. She was the most looks-conscious person I've ever met. Darla didn't just count calories; she counted fractions of calories. She had apps to keep track of her fractions of calories. She'd had a number of cosmetic surgeries by top-notch surgeons. She worked out incessantly, dated guys who were never less than objectively handsome, and never had children. The idea of children was far out of her zone of comfort. Children meant pregnancy, pregnancy meant getting fat, and childrearing meant that she would need to put someone else's interests above her own. Plus, children love sweets, and there could be candy around the house.

As I said, Darla had cheated on Tony. Nonetheless, Tony was totally under her spell. He tried to save their relationship by saving her, which meant having her see me. Our work was a failure. It could not be otherwise, because Darla's goal turned out to be to use me to learn how to do what she had done before, but to do it better and more skillfully. She was planning to take our work and use it to exert even more power and leverage over others. I can count on one hand the number of clients with whom I've called it quits. Darla accounts for one of those extended fingers. I'm sorry, but I can't and won't allow myself to be used that way, even if the client tells me that she or he is making "progress." I have no idea what happened to Darla and Tony afterward. I suspect she's still self-obsessing.

We've talked about how a person's emotional relationship with food can have its roots in childhood. It can also have its roots in any of the frames that we've considered so far. Traumas and injuries can result in using food to soothe the pain. Feeling victimized in life can leave one feeling victimized by food as well. We have all heard people exclaim with profound self-justification, "No matter what I do, I can't lose the weight! I feel like universe is conspiring against me!" Those whose lives are dominated by quandaries can port these quandaries over to the arena of food, because eating becomes a solution to the quandary, or at least an outlet for the discomfort of living with it. If one can't figure out the quandary of a sexless marriage versus separation or divorce, it's not so hard to pad over to the cupboard, take out a box of cookies, and let the power of biology fill both the stomach and the void.

For all these things, food becomes a substitute for dealing with reality. Moreover, it's an acceptable substitute that gets a lot of positive social feedback and commiseration when it is being gained and lost. That said, the fact remains that food and weight are a deflection from the true matters at hand. It is easier and more socially acceptable to focus on losing ten, thirty, or a hundred pounds than it is to deal with what's really going on in a person's life. We can always make the argument to ourselves that we put the weight on; therefore, we can be the ones to take the weight off. Everywhere we look, we see others fighting the same battle. We join the war, for better or for worse, without ever dealing with what's truly going on inside our psychology, our love relationships, our families, and ourselves.

It's impossible to discuss issues of food and sex without spending some time on the topic of plastic surgery, which has advanced now to levels of expertise unheard of twenty or thirty years ago. It has also advanced to a place of complete acceptance in our society, until a person uses that surgery to disfigure himself or herself in some way. Yet the idea that the doctor can do what can't be done otherwise is not just infinitely appealing to the consumer, but accepted by the society at large. We are completely used to the idea of media figures, politicians, actors, and friends disappearing for a week or two, and returning reshaped, resculpted, and looking twenty years younger. When that becomes a norm in a culture like ours, abstaining from plastic surgery can make a person seem unreasonable.

My feelings on this phenomenon are mixed. I had a client named Joseph who suffered from gynecomastia – the growth of female-like breasts. When he reached puberty, these breasts became prominent, and he was suffering at the hands of his peers as a result. No amount of anti-bullying training was going to rescue him, either. I brought in his parents and told them point-blank that while as a general rule I prefer for people to reach adulthood before having cosmetic surgery, there are exceptions for physical and psychological necessity. A teen girl with enormous breasts who cries herself to sleep at night because of the unwanted attention of boys and men is a good example. Joseph is another.

Most of us, though, don't have plastic surgery for medical reasons. We have it to make ourselves look better. In the area of weight loss, for example, gastric bypass and lap-band surgery are the new normal, despite the fact that the medical evidence shows an in-shape person who carries a lot of weight is in better medical shape than a skinny out-of-shape person. That may be the medical evidence, but it is not the evidence that registers in our heads when we look at ourselves in the mirror and ask, "Am I desirable?"

Far be it for me to denigrate the concept of desirability. I vote yes. The danger with cosmetic surgery, though, is the danger posed by desire itself. If one surgery can increase a person's self-assessed desirability rating by a certain percentage, then how much could a second surgery do? Or a third? At what point does it stop, and when are we to be satisfied with the result?

I had a client who had had three surgeries in five years; each one came after she broke up with a boyfriend. My client Candace went for a tummy tuck within a month of having her fifth child instead of allowing her body to heal naturally. I had no particular objection to the tummy tuck. I did object to her not following the natural course of recovery.

There's an old joke about a woman who has lost her watch at night. Her friend finds her looking for the watch under a street lamp. The friend asks if the woman lost her watch under that street lamp. The woman says no, she doesn't know where she lost the watch. The friend then asks, "Why are you looking for the watch here, then? It's probably not even here."

The woman turns to her friend, serious as can be. "True. But here, there's more light!"

Plastic surgery in general, and weight-loss surgery in particular, are like the streetlamp in the joke. Looking for the answer to our weight issues under the streetlamp of bariatric surgery, dieting, and obsessing about food is doomed to fail. Self-medicating with any substance, whether that substance is alcohol, food, drugs, or sex, is a symptom of, and an expression of, larger problems. Quite often, if we change the circumstance that's leading to the problem, or change the emotional relationship with the substance, the need to self-medicate will wither like a weed that gets no water. The issue is not that we don't know what to do about food and weight on a practical level. A person needs to have been living in a monastery for the past three decades without media or communication to not know that a combination of diet and exercise, along with moderation in eating, is the route to a body that he or she can live with. Education is not so much the issue. Forming a healthy emotional relationship with food, and getting extricated from the destructive frames that govern how we look at the world, is the issue. It can be done, and each of us is just the person to do it.

LEVEL OF EXISTENCE #3:
YOU AND YOUR RELATIONSHIPS

Human life is dependent on human relationships. Literally, and figuratively.

There are few species in the animal kingdom that come to maturity as slowly as human beings. It takes us ten or more years to reach sexual maturity, and many more years than that to be able to function as thinking and breathing adults. The law takes this process into account, making age eighteen the age of majority. If a person is underage, it is presumed that she or he is under the care of his or her parents, and cannot make many decisions about his or her life. For example, all contracts entered into by minors are voidable. Judging from the conduct of more than one person in my office – I am sure that my experience is duplicated in your own life, and illuminated almost anytime you take to the road to drive from Point A to Point B – I sometimes wonder whether the age of majority should be age forty, fifty, or more.

The very lives of infants and young children are dependent on their relationships with others. Infants cannot survive without care. An uncared-for infant is the subject of societal horror. It is almost as if we can see ourselves in that baby's helplessness. We know that if the baby is not fed, clothed, sheltered, and looked after, he or she is more helpless than a newborn kitten. We also know that the baby will need nurturance for many years to come; maturity and self-sufficiency take a long time to develop. Few things fill us with as much anger as a news story about an adult who exploits children for his or her own selfish needs, whether those needs are financial, sexual, or economic. It is bad enough when an adult acts criminally toward another adult. When that same adult's object of criminality is a minor, every vindictive instinct in our souls gets triggered. This is why child molesters typically have a very difficult time in prison. Their mistreatment at the hands of guards or other prisoners tends to evoke very little empathy or sympathy from anyone.

Fortunately, most human relationships are not exploitative. They have as much potential for good as they do for harm. Relationships, in fact, are what make our essential humanity possible. Without relationships, morality is impossible. Without relationships, love is a theoretical concept, instead of a blessed reality in our lives. Without relationships, there would be nothing to say and even less to discuss. Without relationships, civility, philosophy, and creativity would be useless concepts. Without relationships, sexuality would be remarkably unsatisfying.

Relationships begin to happen from the moment we come into the world. Our first relationships have their origins in sex and DNA, as we bond to our first caregivers. There are, of course, exceptions, as with orphaned or abandoned children who are raised by non-blood relatives. For most of us, though, our first relationships are forged with our mothers and fathers, and then our sisters, brothers, grandparents, aunts, uncles, and cousins. Those relationships are the templates for all others. They tend to be the relationships by which all others are judged. No wonder, then, that families have such primacy in our thinking and emotional reactivity, whether we embrace them, reject them, or are someplace in between. The earliest stories in the Bible are family stories – Cain and Abel, Abraham and Sarah and Isaac, Jacob and Esau, and then Jacob, Leah, Rachel and their children. It is only after the going down to Egypt, and Pharaoh's embrace of Joseph after Joseph was abandoned by his brothers, that the Genesis story expands, setting the stage for the emergence of Moses as a leader of the Hebrew people. Without the family foundations of the most central text of our time, there would be no story to tell.

From our roots in the family, our relationships branch out. When we reach puberty, sexuality adds a variable to relationships that didn't exist before; we embrace it, tolerate it, or wall it off and forbid it. No matter what we do with it, sexuality is something of an elephant in the room that must be reckoned with. Failure to reckon with sex has wrecked careers and led to presidential impeachments, as well as provided fodder for the juiciest of media scandals. It is worth nothing that one of the unanticipated consequences of the normalization of homosexuality is that sexuality will be less assumed than ever. That is, we may be unsure about whether a same-sex relationship carries the possibility of sexual undertones until we get to know our relationship partners.

At about the same time that sexuality gets introduced, the boundaries of our relationships expand. More than ever, we become not just part of a family and a network of friendships, but also part of a series of communities. These communities can be as ordinary as our first middle-school soccer team, or as profound as our churches and synagogues. We form them in education and at camp. It is often though religious organizations, in fact, that we get our first taste of what it means to be part of a larger community. All active members of The Church of Jesus Christ of Latter-day Saints, for instance, would tell you of their kinship with and affinity for church members who live half a world away. Same thing with our Jewish friends, whose identification with a worldwide people has been at the root of such good for the world, as well as such a target of evil. Yet one doesn't have to be part of a faith community to feel a connection to humanity in the largest sense. We are all part of a global community, as we float on this marvelous planet through the heavens.

By the time we're adults, we're all involved in a tangled web of relationships. Friendship, love, family, community, employment, church...the list of relationships goes on. These relationships have the potential to support us like a sturdy framework. Yet there's also a dark side. The frame can also collapse around us or tighten and pull us apart like some sort of medieval torture device. When either of these things occurs, we lose both the positive parts of the relationships and a piece of ourselves.

The plus side of a significant framework is accountability. In the LDS world, the Orthodox Jewish world, the observant Catholic world, and the fundamentalist Christian world, you're accountable to a whole lot of people, and a whole lot of people are watching you. That can help you lead a virtuous life. It can also be incredibly stifling. I had a client report to me that he saw a bearded, black-clothed, Hasidic Jew in a strip club. I am less interested in the apparent hypocrisy of this man than in the all-too-real human struggle of what was happening. Probably, the man realized that no one else from his sect would see him there, and that being in that place was a way of asserting his independence. Could there have been a healthier outlet for this man? I am not in a position to judge. I would imagine that in the man's hyper-accountable world, there is not much that one can do in private, besides praying or studying, which would not call for a lie.

The largest framework issue that I see now in non-religious communities is failure to launch. That is, the way that many Millennials get locked in a dance with their parents that does little to differentiate parent from the newly adult child. The degree of parental involvement in their children's lives now, compared to the degree of involvement of the generations of their parents and grandparents, is staggering. It is a throwback, in some ways, to the first half of the twentieth century, when our great grandparents and great-great grandparents were deeply involved in their children's lives well into adulthood. To be realistic, one should not underestimate the macro-economic factors pushing parents and adult children under the same roof. It's hard to get a job out there, even for college graduates. Student loans are crushing. The idea of earning a living wage with just a high school diploma is a fantasy. Even so, parents are aware of what's going on with their children, and in communication with them, more than ever before. Our electronic age leads too often to communication gridlock that is more like a web of entrapment.

I had a family in my practice recently that is a good example of this enmeshment. The parents are professionals. The father is a doctor, the mother a schoolteacher. They have one child at home who's twenty-four and in graduate school, and another, age sixteen, who's in high school. The texts between parents and children fly on a regular basis – dozens of them a day. The father admitted to intervening with a graduate-school professor when the older child had an academic issue. The mother avows that she will do everything and anything she can to make sure that her teen daughter does not go through the same adolescent struggles that she went through. She regularly gives advice on social matters. She and her daughter follow each other on Twitter and are Facebook friends. She has gone so far as to write one of her daughter's papers to avoid the girl getting a bad grade. She justifies it in her own mind by saying that in the long run, the bad grade will hurt the daughter more than the cheating. Far be it for anyone to say that parents should not maintain communication with their children. Children who talk with their parents are fortunate. But the lack of demarcation between parents and children can lead to children's involvement in their lives in an unhealthy way, and vice-versa. Boundaries matter, lest the parent emotionally manipulate the child for selfish ends. Boundaries also demarcate right from wrong.

It is fair to say that the most enduring tension of relationships is between the need for the connection and the need for autonomy. We have all seen relationships that can own us and trap us. We have also seen ourselves, at different parts of our lives, viewing and reacting to our relationships differently. Sometimes the self is primary. Sometimes, the couple is primary. Sometimes a community or the nation is primary, as when we're called collectively to fight a just war. What can be baffling and confusing is how even apparently consistent relationships make changing demands on us and our autonomy. Relations are nothing if not fluid.

Expecting them to be tomorrow one hundred percent as they are today is not a reasonable expectation.

Once again, our upbringing can be the enemy here. As I wrote previously, at the time when we are at our mother's breast, or at the bottle, life is perfect and enduring. The baby has no concept that she or he will be hungry again in a few hours, or any concept that for the mother involved, this precise moment of nursing might be less than convenient. All our infant selves want and need is to be held and fed. That's our earliest model of a relationship. Yet to port over that babyish – in the strictest sense of the word! – view of relationships to the adult world is to try to re-create the impossible. It is like a belief in Santa Claus. There are times when a core belief in Santa can be comforting, but as adults, we know it is a construct that exists to serve a purpose that is not connected to reality. Similarly, to believe that our love relationships, family relationships, and friendships can ever achieve the same kind of homeostasis as the baby and the mother is to believe in a myth. Movies and television might perpetuate the mythology – there's a reason that myths have been popular as long as there have been people to create them – but it is mythology nonetheless. If you're upset about some aspect of your relationships? If you're not calm in them? If there's uncertainty and a degree of anxiety? If there's a change today from how thing were yesterday? All we should be saying is "Welcome to the club!"

Relationships require you to have a solid core. It's only through your own solid core that you will be able to maintain your own autonomy, and it is only through the maintaining of autonomy that the relationship will be beneficial both for you and the other person or people in that relationship. The starting place for the development of a solid core is in knowing yourself, and making conscious decisions about whose opinions are going to matter to us. We complain about people who judge us, but judgment is part of life. In fact, the motto of real life might be, "I think, therefore I judge." The biblical injunction of "Let he who is without sin cast the first stone" is far more about grace, forgiveness, and appropriate punishment than it is about not being judgmental. A crime is a crime, after all.

Some judgments matter to us. Some opinions held by others do not. When we allow people to make judgments that we take to heart, we're making ourselves terribly vulnerable. Do not get me wrong: I believe that voluntarily making ourselves vulnerable to some people is one of the incredible strengths of a positive relationship. A husband and wife cannot function emotionally if they do not permit themselves to feel vulnerable with their partner. Yet too much vulnerability means that we're like a hatchery fish dumped into a pond. That is, the first flashy thing we see? We're hooked.

My counsel to my clients is to seek to become *unhookable*. Unhookable does not mean being unapproachable emotionally, or becoming an emotional automaton. What it does mean is that the person has moved from a place of enmeshment to a place of emotional autonomy, where the vagaries of life and the manipulations of others do not provoke an automatic response. Instead, the natural response becomes to listen and observe, and then respond. The confounding thing about the idea of maintaining a position of unhookability is that it runs counter to the best of our instincts when we evolve to a place of genuine maturity. When we have reached a place of caring, compassion, and empathy, we can be as vulnerable to being hooked into a situation as when we are operating out of a place of fear and being subject to manipulation.

My mentor Stephen Covey always said that it takes twenty minutes after an interruption to get a person back into a focused position to do his work. After months of an open-door policy at his office, and the inevitable interruptions that came with it, he finally put a note on his door: "Hello. I am unavailable to be seen. I am available for consultation between the hours of noon and one. Be brief. I am sorry, but your emergency is not my emergency." Covey's attitude may seem callous, but it isn't. He is doing his best to do his own job, in addition to that of his staff. If he didn't do his own job, his staff wouldn't have jobs. He doesn't want to be hooked.

I think of my client Lola, who is really a remarkable woman. She is in her thirties, and has come out of the most rugged background imaginable to build a complete life for herself. Her parents were immigrants who never got past fifth grade. She has several brothers and sisters. The vast majority of them are involved in drugs, criminal activity, or worse. Lola is the second from the oldest. How she managed to escape from this situation is beyond my best comprehension. She not only graduated from high school, but also managed to get some college under her belt. She waitressed at what they call in the South a meat-and-three from the time she was old enough to work, and became so popular with the customers that some would call to make sure that Lola was working before they would come in for meal. She got married to a good man. This was a fellow who worked construction, and when he said he was playing golf, he was actually on the course.

The problem for Lola was that she was the only competent one in her family of origin, and everyone else knew it. She was the only solvent one, too. Her family leaned on her all the time, and she felt something like survivor's guilt for having achieved when the rest of them did not. All family-of-origin members were problematic for her at various times, but none more than her sister Graciela, who was a serious methamphetamine addict. As is too often the case with self-destructive addicts, she was also the mother of two young children. Graciela constantly was asking Lola for assistance, for money, for support, for help…and Lola found it nearly impossible to say no. She feared a "no" would hurt the children, whom she considered to be innocent.

The worst was on an autumn night when Lola received a call from an all-night corner market. Her sister was hysterical. Her building was on fire. The children were inside. She had already called emergency services. Could Lola please come help her – *now?!*

Lola did what anyone would do. She went and got her hysterical sister, and rushed back to the supposedly burning building. The fire department was already there, with the firefighters wearing the knowing grim smiles of public-sector workers summoned yet again to an imaginary call by people whose brains are too addled by drugs to tell what is real and what isn't. There was no fire. There was no emergency. Everything was fine. Well, not everything – Graciela had hooked Lola yet again, and Lola felt powerless to stop it.

Every time Lola made an effort to decouple, Graciela would make maximum effort to be reasonable. She would come to Lola's house looking presentable, but then would be discovered to have been going through the family drawers in search of cash. There were long discussions between Lola and her sympathetic husband about what do. Graciela was poisoning everything she touched, including Lola. Lola's health began to suffer, her marriage began to suffer, and her children began to suffer. In her effort to save Graciela and especially Graciela's children, she had reached a place where she could not save herself.

We had long discussions about measuring her responses. The conversations worked on an intellectual level, but it was hard to get them to work as well on an emotional level. The feelings were too strong. What did work for her was a series of hypotheticals, where we would war-game actions that might be taken by her sister, and similarly war-game her responses. What was most powerful and helpful in these enactments was that I was the one who reminded her of the cost of every action and reaction to Lola and the people around her. Her frame of analysis, when she ran through the calculus of the possibilities, was to focus on the hope of what was be accomplished by her mission, instead of what the actual cost would be, whether the hope was attained or not.

I see issues of hookability and inextricability with other partners of addicts, even after the partnership might have ended. The presence of children from the partnership is very serious glue. It is common, in situations of a divorce that left children behind, for the addict to still look to the divorced partner for help in a crisis, and nearly impossible for the divorced spouse not to say, "Well, he is the father of my kid. Of course I have to step in!" Issues of hookability and unhookability often arise with the loved ones of those in twelve-step programs. Much of the doctrine of Al-Anon is to help people deal with the sense of responsibility that we call feel for others who are in crisis. Normally, as I said before, the sense of responsibility is a sign of being a mature and evolved person, of not being wrapped up in oneself. But with an addicted loved one who has let their life or disease spiral into a world of hurt, the word "responsible" has to be interpreted in a broader sense. You can't be responsible for another if it means that you are going to shirk your responsibilities to yourself and others. I know of ex-spouses of alcoholics who still swoop in to assist them ten or more years after a divorce, justifying their conduct on the grounds that the alcoholic is the parent of their child. The second piece is true, but it does not make a rational case for the first.

There are serious issues of hookability with aging and ailing parents. Elderly parents go into child mode. They need care the way that children need care. They need management. The status quo of the marriage, in which the partners would care for each other, no longer works. Either one member of the couple – typically the woman – will become the primary caregiver, or neither partner is capable of doing the work.

I can't tell you how many marriages get stressed over this. It is emotionally fraught, not the least of which is because dealing with the issues also means that we are staring in the face of our own mortalities. There are a few practical things that we can do about this. We can discuss living wills with our parents while they are still healthy and competent – meaning, when they are in their sixties, not in their eighties. We can figure out an advance health directive. We can talk with our siblings about who should be making the most difficult decisions at the end, and having that talk with our parents, too. They may have things to say on that score, too.

There is a double unhook that needs to happen here. The aging parent has to unhook from the idea that they are going to live forever, and that nothing is going to happen to them – or if it does happen, it's going to be like in the movies. Unfortunately, it almost never happens like in the movies. It is uncertain and always frightfully expensive, and the parent needs to unhook from the fantasy that he or she will be able to move into a child's home and turn into some elderly version of *Father (or Mother) Knows Best*. That's not the reality. Not in most cases, anyway.

From the kids' point of view, the issues are different. Ideally, the wise elderly parent will raise these issues first, but frankly, most of the time? They don't want to upset their children. So, it is up to the children to do it. As far as those children are concerned, it is reasonable for the adult kids to have different points of view on handling issues of aging parents. In my mind, the children who live on the scene should be deferred to, as opposed to the child who lives a thousand miles away. Those who are away should support the ones who are there. They should do everything they can to help. They can take advantage of federal and state leave policies. If they can contribute more economically, they should. And they should be willing to spell their siblings so that they can take a break. And even then, it's going to be hard. Sickness, death, and dying always are. The best we can hope for is that life is long and the end is merciful.

Hookability is also an issue between parents and their children. There is a saying that "A parent is only as happy as her least-happy child," and I can tell you from personal experience that there is great wisdom in the aphorism. It's a delicate balance that must be achieved by any parent: the balance between wanting to swoop in and take away a child's discomfort, versus letting the child suffer in the aftermath or anticipation of whatever the issue is. Any parent who has ever been taken aside by their fourth grader and told about a long-ago-assigned project on the night before it is due knows exactly what I'm talking about.

So. The question this leads us to is, what does a woman do when she finds herself to be hookable? What is the right course of action when her natural intuitiveness and caring lead her toward a hooked situation with any person? The answer is first to be willing to recognize this character trait, and then to get some counsel. I would never fix a hole in my wall if I didn't know what I was doing. Why would I try to fix a hole in my life if I had the same deficit?

I think about my client Joseph. When he came to me, he was in his late thirties, and unmarried. This was one of the most intellectually powerful men I've ever met – a genius, really. He'd been a superb student right through graduate school, with a love for academics. He was a "techie," with a lucrative job writing code for a software company. He lived in front of a screen, and was incredibly skilled at everything having to do with technology. He was an interesting guy, quite possibly somewhere on what's now fashionably referred to as the autism spectrum. What he didn't have were a lot of social skills, or any knack for making a relationship with a woman work. That wouldn't have been so bad if he was a typical nerd happier with online relationships than with real ones. Not my Joseph, though. Oh, no. That would be too easy. Isn't it true that we always want what we're not naturally good at? Joseph wanted to be a parent, to be married, to have a family. It was up to me to help him.

The work was arduous, but we figured out his pattern. There was something in his life that had him hooked, and he had to become unhooked. It sounds strange, and impossible, but it is true that for Joe, the thing that had him hooked was criticism. Any criticism. He just couldn't take it. Now, the easy part was identifying that Joseph had been raised by hypercritical parents. That was no problem. The problem was how to respond to Joseph's heartfelt, "I know what the *what* is now. What I don't know is what to do about it."

We worked on the "what" in session after session, with a man who was so shy and introverted that he was terrified of connection for fear of criticism from his partner. I set out to test him in the controlled environment of my office. I tried to create, literally and figuratively, experiences that would frighten him, and show him that his fear could be managed. Frankly, I beat him up emotionally in the office. It was playacting; he knew it, and I knew it, so there was no harm done. It was not all that different from how people with a fear of flying are conditioned to be able to take a flight on a plane. Essentially, I worked to get Joseph to live with the idea of feeling bad without being completely flooded and "hooked." At the same time, I tried to normalize the experience for him.

The story of Joseph has a happy ending. He worked through this with me, and then moved to Silicon Valley, married, and had two children. He never became a particularly connected human being who put a premium on talk and emotional openness. He never learned to see the value of criticism, but at least it didn't shatter him. Fortunately, he married a woman who was a lot like he was. She was a scientist who loved her laboratory. They're still married.

What I loved most about working with Joseph was watching his courage grow. We all have our vulnerabilities. We tend to go through the same emotional crucibles again and again, fighting those vulnerabilities all the way. Joseph did that, too. But as he came to accept what frightened him, and to see that it would not kill him, he was able to unhook himself.

There are whole professions out there where the professional is going to be confronted by what frightens them: the firefighters, the soldiers, the policemen… The more they train, the more they inhabit the experience of the scary; the better prepared they are when the scary becomes real. In their training, they do what I did with Joseph. They confront the scary and have it presented to them in different ways. They read about it, watch movies about it, simulate it, and put it inside themselves. No one knows what way of learning is going to be the way that connects, and ultimately unhooks us.

Becoming unhookable does not mean that one should never voluntarily be vulnerable. Nor does being unhookable mean that there are no responsibilities beyond oneself. What it does mean is that vulnerability should be voluntary and considered, instead of involuntary and expected. Unhookability is not about isolating oneself. There are many families out there that a family member might see as toxic; where there's an oppressor as part of the family matrix who makes vulnerability unthinkable and even psychologically dangerous. Being unhookable also doesn't mean never seeing that family member ever again – skipping birthdays, weddings, and funerals. Instead, a voluntary and considered approach to the family matrix can usually de-fang that person in our lives without a complete cut-off of contact.

By moving to a place where we are unhookable, we are essentially making ourselves *bulletproof*. This is another useful term I use that can be easily misunderstood. Being bulletproof doesn't mean that we can't hear criticism from others, and take that criticism to heart. The best love relationships will have devastating conversations from time to time, with the partners extraordinarily honest with each other. That honesty is not always positive. What bulletproof does mean is that we are not vulnerable to bullets coming from those whose opinions do not matter to us. It is like we have an emotional flak jacket that we can don, like the one I helped Joseph construct for himself.

Every relationship evolves and develops, just as we develop from dependence to independence. We develop physically, emotionally, mentally, financially, and even spiritually. The disquiet in so many relationships comes from our assessing our current level of autonomy and independence, and then balancing it against the vulnerability that the particular relationship requires. This struggle and weighing process is innate. If there is one common theme in assessing whom we want to be vulnerable with in our relationships, it is that the relationship needs to arise from a place of maturity. I often counsel new couples not to marry until both partners are as independent as possible from their family of origin. A couple where one partner is still being supported financially by the parents is not a couple that is beginning from a place of sure-footed independence. Self-chosen interdependence best comes from a prior position of independence. There are just too many opportunities for one or the other partner to be subjected to outside influence when they are not standing on their own two feet when the marriage begins.

I also counsel couples to take a close look at each other's functionality heading into the marriage. I had a couple several years ago – he was a scientist at a major university physics program, and she was a real-estate agent. They were a beautiful young couple, and confessed with some pride that they had an amazing sex life. I had no reason to think that they were exaggerating. Then I started asking them about the day-to-day details of their couple life. They were living together, so they already had a pattern. Here's what it came down to: He lived in the laboratory, and she did everything else. She cooked, she took care of the car, and she took care of their social life. He made important discoveries, and she handled all the details. When I suggested that this might not be the best possible balance for the long run, she looked at me askance – in disbelief, really. His work was for the benefit of mankind and science, she told me. He had won major prizes! Anyone can sell real estate, but not everyone can do physics at the highest levels. I remember him nodding in agreement. When I asked him how he felt about this division of labor, he told me he was fine with it. He wasn't a very detail-oriented person anyway, except in the realm of quantum mechanics. There, he could remember everything. But he couldn't remember to get the oil changed, or to put snow tires on the car, or that his wife had asked him to call the cable company because HBO wasn't coming in anymore.

I sounded some cautionary notes about how this balance might be acceptable now in the present, but unacceptable in the future. They ignored my counsel. I didn't see them again for five years. That's when the woman returned to me, having newly separated from her scientist husband and firmly committed to a divorce.

"You were right," she told me.

What could I say besides, "I know"?

Women want a man, not a boy. Men want a woman, not a girl. A woman with a man *works*. In a heterosexual coupling, any other combination fails. It might not fail in the early days of great sex and gaga eyes, but it will fail as surely as an engine without oil will fail. It can be seductive to be the one in a relationship on whom the functionality of the relationship depends, but it is also tiring as all get-out, and a resentment factory. It is hard to see the upcoming crash-and-burn at the beginning, looking forward, but the wreckage can't missed at the painful end, looking backward. When it comes to relationships, don't be seduced. And whatever you do? For your own sake, don't seduce yourself.

LEVEL OF EXISTENCE #4:
PHYSICAL AND NON-PHYSICAL UNIVERSE

In a world that's dominated by media, technology, tweets, and texts, in a world where someone leaving us an actual voicemail is seen as an imposition, in a world where our smartphones let us water our lawns, program our DVRs, lock our cars, and watch real-time streamed video of events happening on the other side of the planet, it's easy to lose sight of the fact that we're living real lives, governed by real laws of physics and nature. So many of us have become experts at managing our electronic hardware, but are beyond klutzy when it comes to the nuts and bolts of day-to-day life.

When I refer to the physical universe, I am talking about living things that have an actual physicality. We humans are a prime example. At our roots, we are physical beings as well as psychological beings. Those great brains we have can't function at optimal capacity until and unless we take care of our physical selves. Our minds and our bodies are connected in ways that are easy to overlook. Neglect one, and the other suffers.

When people present with depression, for example, some of the first advice that any doctor or psychotherapist will give is to worry less about what's happening in the brain and think more about what the person is doing from the nose down. In my experience with depressed clients, there are some persistent commonalities. Usually the depressed person has been dealing with a loss or an upset for a long duration. They have something they have not been able to resolve in their past and it is causing them to lose their life force. Another recurrent reason for depression is that the patient is dealing with failed life dreams. When we put all we have into a dream and it doesn't happen, we get depressed. Failed dreams are losses serious enough to cause depression and even suicidal thoughts. When we spend all we have in pursuit of a goal, and the goal doesn't happen, it can devastate us personally and leave us empty. Yet at the same time, it is critical to have a future we are looking forward to, and a goal or goal that we are seeking. Without striving, life gets bleak. The depression that results has both physical and psychological components. To neglect the physical components is to neglect half the equation.

Depression is physically ugly. When Roger came to my office, he was a mess. This was a guy in his late twenties, with unkempt hair, who was unshaven, and – from the aroma wafting toward me – largely un-showered; not necessarily the kind of person anyone would want to be around. What was shocking was that I had known him for ten years, and remembered that he had been a fine young man. He was the eldest son of a friend. He had been a star in high school: athlete, scholar, volunteer, creative, great friend, the whole nine yards.

When he finished high school, Roger joined the military so he could support the country's efforts in Afghanistan and Iraq. He had done tours of duty in both places. When he came home from the service, he was an absolute disaster. He had been traumatized by the fighting, by the uncertainty of the mission, and by the corruption that he saw in the societies of the people for whom he and his buddies were ready to fight and die.

Roger presented himself to me in a state of nihilistic anomie, and it was horrendous. I remember how, in his first session, he kept biting his fingernails and spitting the detritus on my floor. It was everything I could to control my shock and my pity, as well as my annoyance at being baited. That his mother was paying for his work with me made it even more difficult. I tried to stay cool while he ignored me, covered my floor with his fingernail chewings, and essentially rubbed my nose in his scat. Finally, I knew I had to do something to shock him out of this complacency, while letting him know, at the same time, that I could empathize with his pain. I grabbed a notebook and slammed it down on my desk. The sound reverberated through my office like a pistol shot.

"You're here for a reason!" I fairly shouted. "I can see that, and you can see that. But you're not going to come in here, wasting my time and your mother's money, so get the hell out of here and don't come back with a shower and a shave!"

He stood wordlessly and departed. I wondered whether I would have to tell his mother that I had failed. When I did talk to her later, she was noncommittal. Maybe I'd done the right thing, she allowed. But maybe I'd also been impulsive and foolish. I have to say that for two long weeks, I wasn't sure myself.

Two weeks later, Roger called me to apologize. When he came back to my office, he was clean-shaven, showered, and ready to talk. And talk we did. I did marathon sessions with him, always careful not to let him veer into victim mode, but always listening to the stories of the traumas that he'd faced and the disappointment in life that he felt. I don't recommend that husbands and wives do this marathon-talk thing with each other, by the way. Sixty minutes is normally the max that a person can attune him or herself for a highly emotional discussion. For Roger, though, his story needed to be fully aired. It took seven and a half hours. We brought in food and drink. I had very little to say. I tried to live with what he was saying, imagine his feelings, and understand his perspective. Once I could understand, I could help. If I couldn't understand, then I would be literally helpless, and Roger would have one more disappointment on which to hang his sadness. In short, my goal was not to wreck the work before it could even begin.

My patience was rewarded. It took a fair number of sessions, but Roger is back to where he wants to be. He's still in the military, by the way. His love for our country is that great. He was able to put his disappointments in perspective and find a way to continue to serve. It's one of the greatest comeback stories I've ever seen.

It is worth pointing out that Roger's return to himself was accomplished without Celexa or Prozac. No drugs, in fact. Instead, the return began with his focusing on first things, as all depressed people should do. That is, the person feeling depression should focus on eating healthy, well-balanced, regular meals, even if their appetite is less than regular or more than regular. The suffering person should move their body, whether moving the body means a half-hour walk around the neighborhood or some quality time in the gym. (The latest research indicates that three ten-minute walks at various times during a single day have all the same good effects as a single thirty-minute walk, and maybe even more. When it's time to take a coffee break, put the coffee in a to-go cup and stride around the building.) Finally, the depressed person should make an effort to get some quality sleep, regular healthy meals, moderate exercise, and sleep. Not one of those things has to do with communicating, except for communicating with our bodies.

It's amazing how many cases of depression this kind of refocus can successfully address, but it shouldn't be such a surprise. Physical health leads to mental health; when our bodies aren't functioning the way they should, it's likely to knock our psychological equilibrium off-balance. Life is a lot more fun when we're feeling stable, so we should be conscious of the things that keep us physically stable, since those same things can help us be psychologically stable, too. Eat healthy food that doesn't present our bodies with a host of chemicals that our bodies were never intended to ingest. Drink clean water. That doesn't mean we need super-duper water filters in our homes, but given the choice between a chemically laden diet drink and a glass of water, opt for water most of the time. Diet drinks are a deal with the devil, anyway. They fool our bodies into thinking we're taking in sugar, so our bodies react if there's actual sugar coming into our systems. After a while, when there's no sugar to be had, our hormones stop reacting. Guess what happens after a week of diet-drink consumption when we eat or drink something with actual sugar? You got it. Our bodies fail to recognize it as real, and the pounds get packed on extra as a result.

As with our bodies, so with those of the people around us. Yes, it's important to be focused on our loved ones' self-esteem, but it's just as important to make sure their bodies are getting what they need to function optimally. We can often put something of a check on our depression by worrying about the right things, and not the wrong ones. It's good to worry about not shaming our children, but just as important to worry that they're not getting enough sleep. It's good to worry about our kids' insomnia, but just as important to worry whether they're physically tired enough from their daily activities to sleep. We need to worry about having better communication skills with our partners, but it's a lot easier to communicate over a balanced dinner at the table than over bags of fast food consumed on the fly in our cars, with the communication interrupted by text messages. There is hardly a mother alive who would allow her child to bike without a helmet, or even walk to elementary school without supervision. Yet when it comes to looking out for the health and safety of ourselves, we backslide. What is even more remarkable is how scrupulous we can be about taking care of the physical needs of our pets, but lackadaisical when it comes to taking care of the same needs in ourselves. Just about every pet dog out there gets regular food, water, and exercise. If we took care of ourselves as well as we take care of our pets, we'd all be a lot happier.

My client Bindy is a good example of a depressed person who worries about the wrong things. Her husband had cheated on her. There'd been a knock-down, drag-out fight over it, and for good reason: He'd cheated with his eldest daughter's best friend. But there were two other children in the house who were under the age of fourteen, so Bindy decided that she would keep living with Ryan. And what she's done to cope with the depression of deciding to live with this guy who'd wronged her — and I am not saying at all that she made a flawed decision – is to focus on all kinds of externals. She's a schoolteacher, and so she is zeroed in on the grades of her pupils as well as those of her own children. She wants them to achieve well, look well, and dress well. She spends an inordinate amount of time on homework help, shopping catalogues, and buffing up the kids' college résumés. Meanwhile, the kids are worried sick for their mother, whose depression is palpable. No one is talking about what's really going on, and the status quo continues.

My intervention – it is ongoing – is to get all the people in this family to face the heart and soul of each other, and be present for each other emotionally. Fortunately, it is working. They're eating well, sleeping well, and exercising well. The kids are still on track to go to college. If they don't get into the University of Southern California the first time around, they know that if they do well at another school, they can always transfer.

This sensitivity to the nuts and bolts of the human body needs to extend to the nuts and bolts of daily living. If you drive a car, you know that the vehicle needs regular maintenance. A car can run for quite a while without having its oil changed, its fluids topped up, and its belts replaced, but it can't run forever. Without regular maintenance, that car is going to die a premature death. Without gasoline in the tank, the car isn't going to get you from Point A to Point B, no matter what your best intentions or need to get there. But it's not just the car that needs attention. We need to pay attention to the world that presents itself to us when we get behind the wheel, whether it is the wheel of our car or – I hate to use the phrase, but it makes sense here – the wheel of life.

I had a client come to me when he was sixty years old. This was a tortured man – I could see it from the moment I met him; there was a secret he was carrying that was almost too much to bear. It took several sessions for the whole story to come out. It came out, as these things often do, in spurts, as the client felt safer and safer with me. This was his story: He'd been in a wreck when he had been sixteen years old. He'd been driving, and his father had been in the passenger seat. It was bad weather. He drove into a fog bank and was hit by another car in a head-on. My client walked away, but his father was killed. For five decades, almost, he was wracked by guilt over something for which he was actually guiltless. He was taking responsibility for a bad situation. There was something noble about it, but at the same time, it was killing him emotionally. Finally, I asked him what he might have done differently on that terrible day. Different headlights? Slower speed? Different tires? Would anything from his end have made a difference?

"Nothing," he said sadly. "There was nothing I could have done."

"That's right. But the person who hit you head-on? That person could have done it a whole lot differently. That person was already in the fog. He could have pulled off to the right at a slow speed, and stopped on the shoulder instead of crossing into your lane. Or even gone off the road into a field at slow speed. His car might have gotten scratched. So what?"

That was the turning point in our work.

The greatest thing that we can do to live harmoniously with the physical and non-physical world is to learn from our experiences. Learning from experiences means to develop resourcefulness, flexibility, and awareness of the situation. It also means not wallowing in regret about how a situation may have overwhelmed us in the past, but actually breaking it down and taking something from it for the future. Life is a series of experiences that sharpen us, strengthen us, or break us. It is not what happens to us, but what we do with what happens to us that determines the course of our lives. Let me offer one example for the guys, and then one for the ladies.

Guys first, for a change. It just so happens that my husband is a drag-racing fan. Actually, fan is too mild a word. He's an outright fanatic. I have to admit that I was skeptical the first time he took me to a track to watch, but I've come to appreciate the combination of technology, skill, and downright danger that comes with highly modified vehicles ripping down a quarter-mile track at 300 miles an hour. If you want a place where the laws of physics and nature rule, there's no place quite like a drag strip. It's also one of the most monitored quarter-mile environments out there. The telemetry is astonishing. Every component of every vehicle is tracked and monitored, every "run" is videotaped; there are biometrics on the driver measuring heart rate, blood pressure, oxygen levels, breath rate, etc. Every possible variable is tracked and analyzed, too, right down to wind speed and track temperature.

The best drag racer in the world is John Force. He is a sixteen-time Funny Car Champion and an eighteen-time champion car owner. He has more career victories than anyone in history. Yet John Force and crew gather all of this same information – every single race. The point of all of this data-gathering is not for Force or anyone else to beat himself up when something goes wrong, or even if the car or driver underperforms. It's to analyze the data and correct the mistake in the future so it doesn't happen again. It's the same principle that has even the most successful National

Football League coaches and quarterbacks spending thousands of hours watching game film. They do it so that they can be resourceful, flexible, and aware of the game – in the next game.

We women learn from our experiences, too. While it's in our nature to be more emotional than men, and to want to review the past in order to assign blame, there is one crucial arena in which we are extraordinarily skilled at learning from our experiences and then applying that learning to the future. That arena is the rearing of a newborn.

Baby-raising and baby care is as primal as life can be. The animal kingdom has it easy, because so much is governed by instinct. Sleeping, nursing, cleaning…there is little variation between the way one cat cares for its kittens and another cat cares for its kittens. That's because there's very little variation among kittens. So long as Momma Cat has a food and water supply for herself, and a safe place to shelter the kittens, those kittens are going to be raised to maturity and someday become Momma Cats themselves.

Infants are different because human brains are different. Get six mothers in a room talking about their babies, and you'll get six different reports on the way those infants are in the world. Some are docile; some are on the verge of aggressive. Some sleep like, well, babies through the night, with nary a cry. Others are far more, ahem, vocal. Some eat a lot, some eat moderately, and some are picky at their nursing. Some seem to have good digestive systems; some manufacture enough gas to make the mother want to call in Exxon. There is a school of psychoanalysis that believes that primitive mental states can be identified by observing infants. I suspect the best-trained analyst in the world could not do this as well as the baby's mother. Our job as women is to become attuned to our child.

And attune ourselves we do – through trial and error, by memory, by paying attention to detail. Attuning to our infants is the difference between a good night's sleep for them and for us, and another day of our dragging ourselves through life. Our attunement allows us to know when the cry of a baby is pain from an earache and when the baby is ready to pass gas. It teaches us to get them to the nipple so they can nurse efficiently. We even attune to our own diets, so we modify what we eat to produce milk that is easiest on a baby's stomach. I learned with my own first child how spicy tacos led to stomach problems – not for me, but for my infant. I learned quickly to keep my diet bland, by way of attunement. Every mother attunes, adjusts, and gets better at mothering. Every new mother feels helpless, and at the beginning, everything with the newborn seems exotic, strange, and downright terrifying. Little by little, though, we learn about the baby. We learn which cry is from discomfort, which is from hunger, and which is from emotional longing. We dial in to body language and patterns.

What is heartening about motherhood is that most of us actually cut ourselves some much-needed slack. Rarely do we sit around and beat ourselves up for our earlier naïve baby-rearing errors. How could we not mess up from time to time? We were such rookies! As our baby grows, so do we. We become resourceful, flexible, and remarkably aware of things that non-mothers just would not notice. We are in tune with the physical world as maybe we have never been before. If we are fortunate, we are able to port this attunement over to other aspects of our lives.

Resourcefulness. Flexibility. Awareness. Three skills that make negotiating this crazy thing called life a whole lot easier, and make it a whole lot easier to appreciate how precious and wonderful it is. Take care to take care.

LEVEL OF EXISTENCE #5:
SPIRITUALITY

I t's hard to be spiritual in a world where there's so much judgment about faith and God. That said, without a sense in our souls that the world and universe is larger than ourselves, who are we, really? The great Jewish teacher Hillel, who lived a generation before the birth of Jesus, famously asked, "If I am not for myself, who will be for me? Yet if I only for myself, who am I? And if not now, when?"

It is my belief that there is an innate connection in all of us with the divine and with the universe. This is the reason that so many of us find comfort in praying with our children before they go to bed. We know that so much in life is beyond our control. We know that whether the sun rises or sets is subject to laws beyond our power, made by forces of which we can only dream. Prayer gives us the time and space to acknowledge that we are connected to those larger forces and power. What's just as striking, though, is that children embrace the connection, too. There is nothing as difficult a task as getting a child to do something that the child just does not want to do. Yet few parents run into this roadblock when it comes to bedtime prayers. It is as if children know instinctively the importance of a daily connection – however brief – to the divine.

Where children, and even we adults, tend to rebel is when our conception of the Almighty does not square with the concept of God that is being foisted on us. There is an endless variety of conceptions of the Almighty that are presented by the world's leading faiths, along with endless varieties of misconceptions of how other faiths see their Supreme Being. For example, the typical Christian concept of the God of Moses as being angry and choleric tends to conveniently overlook those instances of great Godly mercy in the Hebrew bible, beginning with the story of the binding of Isaac on Mount Moriah. The Jewish view of God is of a Being of both judgment and compassion. So is the Christian view of God. Few Christians would say that the God who loves us cares not at all about how we treat each other.

In some ways, these varying characterizations of God are harmless. Every faith, denomination, and religious leader is entitled to its own, and his or her own, template for the Almighty. The fact is, a template is just that – a template. Just as a map is not the territory, a template for the Supreme Being is not the Supreme Being. Even calling God by that name is an effort to name the unnamable. Where things break down in an unbeneficial way is when God is brandished as a weapon. People get told that we are going to hell if we don't do what God wants us to do. All of us make mistakes and do ungodly things. Ipso facto, hell must be a big place.

What does God want us to do? The larger principles are clear. We are to treat each other decently. We are to follow basic precepts of decency, most of which overlap from faith to faith. But some faiths worship on Sunday, some worship on Saturday, and some worship on Friday. Which faith has the right day of worship? Your belief depends on your belief as to who has had the true revelation. God gets brandished as a weapon when we are guilt-tripped to obey, lest we be punished. God is also brandished as a weapon when we hear about others' revelations for us – where someone has the audacity to tell us that they have heard a revelation about us in particular, and we are to follow the revelation that they had, or risk the wrath of God.

When God is used as a weapon, we have a natural reaction. We recoil. When we see God used to manipulate and dominate others, we recoil on their behalf. When God is used as a way to denigrate the free will that was established for us in the Garden of Eden story, we rebel at that. There is an oft-told tale about how Satan and Jesus were at the foot of God, talking of how they wanted to approach choice in the world. Satan's plan was to use force. Make humans obey, and when they didn't obey, punish them. When the Hebrew prophet Jonah went to Nineveh, he was actually disappointed that God did not level the city – that the people of Nineveh had actually repented as God had wanted. Jesus, on the other hand, believed in the ongoing free agency of humanity. Spirituality and belief in the Almighty became a choice for people to make. God could make clear the awesomeness of his works, but should not force them into belief.

There is a tremendous tension between these two positions. We know about the primacy of free will and the absolution of forgiveness, yet even the Gospel of Mark talks about the existence of one unforgiveable sin, without specifically defining what that sin might be. Historically, the definition of the word Satan was "accuser." The tension between doing right out of choice, and doing right out of fear, permeates our lives. It actually holds societies together. Yet when God is brandished as a weapon, it becomes less likely that the intended victim of the weapon is going to want to be Godly in his or her heart. That is, they clench when what they are told about God doesn't add up, and in fact it sounds dishonest to them.

It sometimes seems as if there is a charade that we play with children about God. When we suggest to a child that they pray to God for X, Y, and Z, and tell them that God will answer a specific prayer if they pray hard enough, neither we nor the child truly believes it. We don't believe it because of our own closetful of unanswered prayers. Children don't believe it because even at their tender ages, they have experience with injustice. What is injustice, if not unanswered prayer? If the most basic manifestation of God is the Golden Rule of doing unto others what we would want them to do to us, even a child can see that this rule is routinely broken with little apparent consequence to the rule-breaker. What is remarkable is that children don't hold God responsible for these violations. They understand the grant of free will in the stories of Adam and Eve, and Cain and Abel. They may actually understand it better than we do.

The older we get, the more the subjects of God and religion carry baggage for us. Were finding our moment with God simply a matter of finding our way into the woods for a meditative walk, or into a still, quiet room for a few minutes every day to allow ourselves some moments of spiritual connection with humanity and the magnificence of the universe, more people would acknowledge that they were religious. Many of us have these connective moments. Here in Utah, it can happen at the top of Snowbasin or Alta on one of those winter days where it seems we can see clear to Colorado, or at the bottom of a canyon at Capitol Reef that took 150,000,000 years to form – 4/1000ths of an inch a year. It may take place on a moonless night under the expanse of the Milky Way. It could be on a visit to the gravesites of our parents and grandparents, amid the headstones of lives lived for better and for worse. It may be in the cry of a newborn, in the opening of a petunia, in the first rain of spring, and the last leaves of autumn. In all these places, in all these things, we connect with the Divine.

Most of the time, though, that's not where we are expected to explore the realm of the spirit. Instead, our faiths have expectations for us – circles in which we must participate. Religion is bound up in all kinds of circles. Many of these circles offer remarkable support and structure, if we can find our way inside. There is the circle formed by a marriage, when the partners carry a sense of holiness into that union. There is the circle of family, and the circle of local community. There is the circle of our faith in general, if we ascribe to one. Whether we are Mormon or Catholic, Jewish or Muslim, a member of a mainline Christian denomination or an independent church, there is sacrifice of the needs of the self in favor of the needs of the group. In return, the power of the group is there to support us when we need it. Anyone who has been a longtime member of any congregation, and then comes face-to-face with life's inevitable sadness, knows the good that a strong community of faith can do. If we show up for others, others will show up for us.

As good and helpful as faith traditions are, we still need to protect our own personal quest for the spirit. For many of us, our earliest vision of God is our faith's vision, and our earliest version of religion is a kind of tutoring about God. Then, inevitably, cracks appear. Sometimes, the cracks are manageable within the boundaries of that faith. For example, in Los Angeles, the remarkable Rabbi David Wolpe at Sinai Temple preached a sermon a few years back about the exodus of the Jews from Egypt. In that sermon, he offered a stunning proposition that some might call heretical. Wolpe suggested that the biblical exodus might not have an historical basis. Mind you, he was still saying that the text of Hebrew Bible had religious significance. His point was that he was willing to address one of the obvious cracks in the architecture of Judaism; that the archeological evidence might not support the notion of an historical Moses.

While there was controversy in the aftermath of these remarks, Wolpe still leads this synagogue, and remains one of the most respected rabbis in the country. In other faith traditions, leaders and followers alike will harbor opinions and arguments that vary from the mainstream. Some faiths are flexible when it comes to tolerating these opinions. Some are downright rigid. Yet all of us can and do look at God and faith through the prism of our own experience in order to make our own spiritual way in the universe. There are times when that might mean holding our counsel for the sake of peace with friends and family.

Shakespeare famously has Hamlet say, toward the beginning of the play that bears his name, "There are more things in heaven and earth, Horatio, than are dreamt of in your philosophy." Who among us does not believe this to be true? Again and again in my office, people tell me of illogical things that happen to them. A weird push to the wheel of their vehicle as they head off the road. A peculiar feeling in the pit of their stomach about a particular person, with no rational basis for that feeling. A dream that seems to be a message from a loved one who has passed. I listen to these stories in wonder. There is nothing rational about these recounted experiences. Nor do they happen all the time. It seems, too, that they are spread across the whole population of my clients. Neither the most devout nor the most irreligious have a monopoly on these kinds of stories. I admit that there have been things that have happened in my own life that defy rational explanation. They do not shake my confidence in mathematics, physics, medicine, or the certainty that the sun will come up tomorrow. They do get me thinking about how to help myself, and my clients, be open to that which is wondrous.

I believe that there are two components of our spiritual life. One of them is communal, and the other is individual. These two components need to be in relation to each other. One without the other leads to a life out of balance. I had a client named Peter whose life was an individual spiritual journey. Rarely have I encountered anyone who spent as much time in the realm of his senses, and the realm of the spirit. Peter traveled the world in search of spiritual redemption. He went alone to the Holy Land, to walk in Jerusalem where Jesus had walked. He spent time at an ashram in Nepal, meditating in the presence of the Himalayas and various yogi masters. He took classes in Judaism, flirted with Islam, and was constantly reading material with a spiritual and religious bent. He had an encyclopedic knowledge of the Catholic saints. It was all quite stunning and, in many ways, admirable. Yet Peter came to me because he felt isolated – all of this religious interest, and he still felt lonely.

It made sense to me. First of all, there is nothing as humbling as coming to understand the insignificance of mankind in the universe. That understanding could make anyone feel lonely. Second, all of this religious journeying was on his own. Peter committed to nothing that involved others for more than the period of time in which he was comfortable. His stay in the ashram, for example, was forty-five days. He came there when he wanted, and departed when he was ready. He was accountable to no one but himself.

I asked him, "What good is all this questing if, in the end, you're in a community of one?"

He had no good answer. I suggested that maybe it would be in his interest to quest a little less, and connect a little more. Ultimately, he found a home for himself in a Quaker congregation. I think he would have been happy anywhere, really. He just needed to choose one place.

The flip side of Peter was my client Susannah. Susannah was a joiner, an organizer, and a community person. She belonged to an established church, and was one of its stalwarts. She was the constant attendee and the consistent volunteer. People came to count on her presence; she got a great deal of respect for her efforts, too. What Susannah didn't have was any time by herself to connect with God. Church for her was entirely social, with emphasis on the word entirely. She came to me with complaints from her family about how all she could talk of was church, church, church. I suggested that she undertake some activities on her own that would give her the breathing room to talk about God, God, God. If that required some strategic withdrawal from church expectations, I imagined that God would understand. Her partial retreat from her church wasn't easy. It is never easy to back away when others count on you. But for many of us, moderate religious communal time and moderate spiritual individual time is the best kind of balanced and nourishing Godly diet that we can partake of.

God and spirituality, in my opinion, can't happen in isolation. The individual part of spirituality is absolutely important. Meditating alone in one's bedroom is an important way to connect. As the AA people say, prayer and meditation are the way to connect to one's higher power. At the same time, there's nothing in the liturgy that says that prayer and meditation have to be done alone; there's power in groups. The group creates the synergy; the group creates a team effort. When you share in a group, you can expand it. The group can also serve as something of an emotional backstop. Our Jewish friends are particularly good at this on the Day of Atonement, when the prayers of confession of sin are spoken communally and aloud. They don't say, "I have sinned," they say, "we have sinned," and in the communal declaration it becomes a safer environment for the sinner to confess.

At the same time that service to one's God can be done privately, it can also be done communally. In fact, it may have special power when it is done communally. A soup kitchen can't succeed if it's just one person making peanut-butter sandwiches. On the other hand, religious practice can't be entirely communal. It's important for each of us to come to a conception of the Almighty, and with the Universe, in our own way. To think of spirituality as being only communal makes about as much sense as thinking that seven billion people on the planet should all have exactly identical handwriting. Not possible. Not even desirable. We don't all paint the same way, and we don't all have spiritually identical beliefs.

The communal part is the part that churches, synagogues, and mosques do so beautifully. When life crashes into us in those strange, unexpected, and even horrific ways that it can, there is nothing like seeking shelter in a community of those who care about us. When evil manifests, when death descends, when illness becomes part of our days and nights, the caring and love of others can do more than we can do for ourselves. This is the reason that I'm so skeptical of grief counseling. The grieving person doesn't need a counselor. The grieving person needs family and friend who share in a common humanity.

The other component is spiritual. This is not to say that an avowed atheist cannot thrive and prosper, even though that atheist does not have a connection to the universe. And same thing for an agnostic, who professes not to know whether God exists. However, I can tell you from my experience that it is far more difficult, and far easier to skid into a path of existential despair, when absent any kind of spiritual connection to the universe.

Loneliness is a spiritual plague that can eat away at us. Alcoholics Anonymous' *Big Book* talks of addiction not as a biological reality but as a spiritual crisis; the remedy is found in both of the spiritual components I've discussed here. On the individual level, the goal is a spiritual reawakening. On the communal level, the goal is strength in the group that the individual addict cannot otherwise experience. Fortunately, most of us are not addicts, even as life tests our faith on a daily basis – if not in what we personally experience, then in what we watch, or read about, or know about. To respond to those tests, we must all, in our own way, strive to build or maintain a connection to a community of people. For many of us, that happens in our houses of worship. For others, it happens in a club, or a charitable group, or simply in a group of lifelong friends. At the same time, we want to foster those moments and times where we are open to connecting to our intuition, and connecting to life on a spiritual plane. It's humbling in the best possible way, and expanding at the same time. The most brilliant spiritual and religious teachers stress the interconnectedness of all life and all humanity. At those moments when we are at one with the universe, we feel interconnected. That interconnection leads to an emotional generosity that can preclude conflict. It is one of the building blocks of love. Everyone – atheist, agnostic, spiritual, or religious person – believes that more love in the world would be a good idea. Everyone could use more love. Connecting with people, and with the Universe, is the way to grow love.

IDENTITY

To prepare to read this chapter, take thirty seconds and complete the following statement, each time giving a different conclusion to the statement – no more than a few words for each. If it were Superman completing this, for example, his first sentence would be either, "I am from the planet Krypton," or, more likely, "I am a superhero." (It would be interesting if his first response were, "I am vulnerable to Kryptonite.")

I am_____

I am_____

I am_____

Do it ten times.

I just did it.

My sentences were, "I am a mother." "I am a counselor." "I am a wife." "I am a spiritual person." "I am a resident of Utah." Like that.

I imagine that yours are not so different. We define ourselves by our families, our professions, our faiths, our nationalities, our communities, our health, our sexualities…the list goes on and on. Some identities are things that we seek deliberately: policeman, college graduate, mother. Others are roles and identities that are thrust upon us: sufferer of chronic pain, orphan, caretaker, sole breadwinner, spokesperson. The irony is, as good as we are at completing the sentences, naming ourselves, and accounting for our own responsibilities at fitting into those roles, we are less good at understanding how those various roles and identities shape us, our thinking, and our relationships. Getting people to describe how their identities shape them is akin to asking a fish to describe the water in which that fish swims.

Our identities make the world go round. So many of the transactions of life have to do with interacting on the basis of a narrow identity. When I want to fill my tank with gas at a convenience store, and buy a drink to go with my twenty dollars of regular, I have a ritualized transaction with the store clerk. I am a customer, and he or she is the clerk. The clerk takes my money, and gives me permission to take my drink from the store and pump gas in exchange for my payment. We have each given something of value to the other in exchange for something of value. Most of the time that is as far as the relationship goes. Frequently, the clerk and I do not know each other's names. If we do know each other's names, it's because we have a standing relationship as a result of multiple transactions. We might say a simple hello, how are you? We might wish the other a good day, or comment on the weather. More than that practically never happens.

The philosopher Martin Buber said that people have two basic kinds of relationships. There are the relationships that are based on a narrow kind of identity. He called these "I-It" relationships. Then, there are the relationships that are truly two souls coming together. He called those "I-Thou" relationships. While there is clearly more spiritual value in I-Thou than I-It, it is clear that if every relationship were an "I-Thou" relationship, the world could not function. Imagine the ticket-taker at an NBA basketball arena having a long, soul-to-soul conversation with each fan entering for game seven of the NBA finals. Not only would 18,000 fans standing in line be unbelievably upset at the delay, but the ticket-taker would be emotionally exhausted by the time he or she reached the tenth or twelfth customer. The goal of the interaction is to get the fan with a valid ticket into the arena safely and quickly, not to have a long discourse on the meaning of life and love.

That said, our identities do shape our lives. They certainly shape how other people and react to us. The novelist Kurt Vonnegut wrote how, "We are what we pretend to be." To a great extent, it's true. We have all seen the tragic effects that selecting a particular outfit of clothing might have on an observer. Coming into a bank while wearing a stick-up mask, even if it's a practical joke or Halloween, could well result in being shot. Dressing like an urban ghetto gangster or a skinhead, is going to result in people responding as if you are a gangster or a skinhead, even if you are a mild-mannered person who happens to think that shaved heads and shorts worn low enough for underwear to show are hip.

The problem on a personal level happens when our identities shape our actions unconsciously, as they often do. This is particularly common with identities that are thrust upon us – identities that we did not choose. I have a client named Andrea who is the elder sister to five little brothers. They're not so little anymore – the younger is eighteen years old and a football player for a major college program – but through her childhood, she was explicitly and implicitly called on by her parents to help maintain the household. They, as parents, were overwhelmed. Andrea stepped into this identity as a surrogate parent with aplomb and skill. She cooked, cleaned, supervised, mediated, and did anything that her parents asked her to do. Her parents would say that she was an ideal big sister. The problem is, Andrea isn't in that household anymore. She's married, and her husband is sick of her bossiness and need to control the details of his life. When I heard about her family of origin, I wasn't surprised that Andrea was a bossy woman. It should be instructive to all of us: When others aren't happy with the way that we're behaving, before we blame them for being judgmental or difficult, we ought to look at when the behavior in question was a behavior that served us well. When I was able to reframe her childhood experience for her, and she was willing to give up a little control in exchange for a lot of love, Andrea and her husband moved forward.

Identities can collide with each other. For everything that is gained by assuming one identity, something is lost in the sacrifice of another one. For me, the most poignant example of this is in the classic film *Field of Dreams*, where the Burt Lancaster character, Archibald Graham, gave up his identity as a ballplayer in order to assume a different identity as a pediatrician. As a result, he never even got an at-bat in the major leagues. Graham admits to Ray Kinsella (played brilliantly by Kevin Costner) that while he was heartbroken that he never got to swing at a major league pitch, he would have been more heartbroken had he never become a doctor. The moment is poignant because any viewer can relate to it. For everything we gain, there is something lost.

I had a client, Bridgette, who became a cheerleader while in high school. She had a friend from junior high named April. Bridgette the cheerleader abandoned her "loser" friend April to hang out and party with the cheerleaders. We see this all the time with teens, who are try on and discard identities like they're blouses at the Gap, and hurt their friends in the process, Often with adolescents, you'll see things that don't necessarily fit – the party kid who is also a brain and also an athlete. When we start to see kids acting obnoxiously and like brats, it is often a function of teen identities in conflict. They want to be good kids with their parents; they want to be cool kids with their friends. Yet it is almost a given that when a teen starts acting inappropriately, there is some new wrinkle or influence in their lives.

One of the downsides of social media culture is the sheer number of influences or stimuli that can knock a teen off course. When my generation was coming of age, a popular kid had twenty friends. When my children are coming of age, they could have two thousand of them, all electronic. The potential vectors for unproductive conduct are exponentially bigger than a generation ago. Teens have always been subject to social contagion. Arthur Miller wrote eloquently about this in *The Crucible*, couching the contagion in the framework of the Salem witch trials. These days, the activity that jumps from teen to teen is not accusing others of being witches, but accusing them of being sluts. Or it's the phenomenon of cutting, where teens will self-injure by cutting themselves on their arms. Allegedly, it provides a release. In actuality, it provides a public forum for making a spectacle of oneself, which others can either emulate or comment on. In either case, attention is being paid to their new identity as a "cutter."

We adults, in our way, are just as prone to getting lost in identity and losing our centers. I have a client named Brian who was a twenty-something slacker. Kind of lovable, in a way. He was a clown, a goofball, and a serious Major League Soccer fan. It was fine when he was single, but after he got married, his wife couldn't put up with him anymore. (Note to prospective wives: Don't think your perfect love will change your husband in the way you want him to change. It's possible, but it sure isn't likely.)

Brian had a basic job in a bank. Through the fortuitous collision of luck and circumstance, he got a serious promotion to another area of the company. His salary went up by a factor of four. All of a sudden, Brian was making six figures. He could hardly believe it. Rather than being a twenty-something classic slacker with a wife, a baby, and a penchant for borrowing money from his wife's father, he was financially independent.

You never saw such a rapid change in a guy's personality. He went from Mr. Slacker to Mr. Alpha. He bought a Dodge Charger and nice clothes. He tried to join a country club. He became confrontational with anyone and everyone when he felt like he was being treated with anything other than deference. My eureka moment with him was when I realized that Brian had absolutely no guide on how to be as a successful man. He was taking what he'd seen on television shows and movies, ranging from the *Godfather* to *Entourage*, to model his behavior. TV was shaping his identity. Once I got him into the company of better role models, like his wife's father, he was able to pull his life together and become a good person as well as a financially successful one.

Sometimes, the fallout from the grip of a powerful identity is heartbreaking. My client Zack was a man among men at the age of thirty. He was gorgeous, powerful, and as blue collar as blue collar could be. He built skyscrapers – he was the guy who stood on the high beams with very little below him. There were muscles on his muscles. And he could drink, laugh, and carouse with the best of him. To say he was a babe magnet was an understatement.

Zack could have squeezed ten or twenty more years out of this version of his life, but it was not to be. He drank a little too much one night and rolled his pickup truck off a road. He went down a ravine, and into a ditch. He was trapped in his vehicle, and was fortunately spotted the next morning by someone walking their dog; it took a helicopter crew to rescue him. There were three months in a coma, and more time in rehab than he will ever want to remember.

Zack's left side is now atrophied, and he is lucky to be able to get around with a walker. When he came to me, he was physically half the man he used to be. The thing was, he still ran at the mouth, still got into fights, and still wanted to be Mr. Badass Stud. There was something both noble and pathetic in this quest for manhood, but there was nothing functional about getting hit in the face and being unable to chase the person who hit him. The turning point for him was when we were able to find a forum for all his testosterone that could achieve with his body. He found various wheelchair sports much more competitive than he ever imagined, and went on to excel at them.

Lives can change for the better when we begin to understand that identities are not like uniforms we must don whether we like them or not. Instead, identities can be shaped, developed, and made to grow. How we are in an identity at Point A in our lives is not the way that we are to be at Point B, or Point C. We are works in progress within our identities; we can define our identities instead of having them define us. I remember when the country singer Martina McBride came on the scene more than two decades ago. She was a pretty girl with a lovely voice, but there was no indication that she would somehow break out of the pack of other pretty girls with nice voices. Yet she did, by hard work and self-reflection. I don't play golf, but I think of how the finest golfers can finish a round and go straight to the putting green for more practice. As with singers and golfers, so with fathers and mothers, sisters and brothers, husbands and wives, sons and daughters and lovers. If all we ever could ever be is how we are at the start of a journey, taking the journey would be an exercise in futility.

One way to stop identities from leading you blindly is to find other, more mindful icons for your life. Dr. Stephen Covey suggested that we could all be more rational and effective actors if we chose to be guided in our lives by principles rather than by identity. Principles have one clear advantage over identity: They are eternal. An old woman can have the same guiding principles that she had as a child. Principles have another advantage. They are crowd-sourced and battle-tested. They have been debated and re-debated from the time of Adam and Eve. There is an argument to be made that the course of human civilization has been a course of discovering those principles by which to live.

It would be the height of ego and folly for me to suggest to you which principles are going to be the specific ones to guide you. For Covey, a guiding principle is "Seek first to understand, then to be understood." For you, a principle may be, "Leave as light a footprint as you can," or "Live by the Golden Rule." The main thing is to have a series of principled mission statements for your life. Your identities could in fact contribute to those principles and mission statements. "Parent so my children may one day be good parents," is an example of this synergy. The idea is not to scrap your identities. The idea is to understand that though identities develop and are thrust upon us, principles are chosen by us. In that choice comes a gift of a liberated life.

In the end, there is a single identity for all of us. We come from dust, and return to dust. That is the reason that so many religious pilgrims don identical clothing for their pilgrimages: to equalize themselves in the eyes of the Almighty, no matter what their social status, past, or present status. They can be kings or they can be paupers, but from the outside, it is impossible to give them an identity other than being a pilgrim. On the Jewish Day of Atonement, some members of that faith attend synagogue wearing the same simple white cotton robe in which they will be buried. It is as if they are making a rehearsal of their own demise. When Christians are baptized by immersion, at the moment that they are immersed, they are all equal in their identity.

It is one of the ironies of life that death and the contemplation of it can bring us back to the essence of ourselves. I have often seen people in mourning undergo what seems to be wholesale personality change for the better. The narcissistic become other-directed. The hyperactive find moments of contemplation. The talkative listen. The listeners share their feelings. All of them – and all of us – come to realize that when it is said and done, we will be judged and remembered not for our identities, and not for our achievements in the moment, but for our legacies.

LEGACY AND RULES TO LIVE BY

L ife must be lived from three points of view.

There is the point of view of the *now*. How are we feeling *now*? What are our immediate needs *now*? How are we feeling now, in this moment? What are we doing now, at this instant? What are our responsibilities at this tick of the clock? How do our husbands, wives, children, loved ones, and communities perceive us at this particular moment in time? In this instant, do we have those life necessities that make us feel safe – is there food, clothing, health, shelter, sex, faith, or are we floundering or aching in one or more of those areas? The *now* is always changing, but also always pressing. It is the immediate driver of our lives, as it should be. The now is what keeps our hearts beating and our lives moving forward.

There is the point of view of the future. The concept is complex. There is the immediate future, the intermediate future, and the distant future. We humans are alone in the animal kingdom is our ability to see and plan for intricate and hypothetical what-ifs. It is often said that a plan of battle doesn't survive the first shot of a war, but that phrase is more hyperbole than true. Plans make the world go 'round. We groom ourselves not just to get out the door in the morning so we can go to work, but also so that we might meet a partner and fall in love; we have a work and family life that we hope will be satisfying; we eat, drink and exercise today so that our health may be vibrant in ten, twenty, or fifty years; and we place limits on what we consume in the now so that we can have more of it available if we need it in the "then." Squirrels may gather nuts in the summer and store them for the winter, but only humans can launch a rocket ship with a particular understanding of physics, telemetry, rocketry, and navigation, so that the payload will rendezvous and orbit another planet and then explore it. A mission like the Curiosity Mars rover is human planning and future thinking at its finest. While it is true that the best laid plans of mice and men go astray, we nonetheless look forward.

Finally, there is the looking backward. We people have a remarkable capacity for memory; for fitting pieces together in a way that makes sense, and for creating memories and legacies for themselves that live on long after our time on what Shakespeare called this "mortal coil" is gone. Legacies are what exist when we are gone. In non-religious terms, they are the way that we achieve a kind of immortality here on earth even when our days have reached their end. Our knowledge of what happens between mankind and after our deaths is a matter of scripture, faith, belief, and interpretation. What happens between people after our deaths is a matter of our legacies.

There is a fascinating duality to the concept of legacy, in that our legacies are both public and private. Public legacies are the permanent things we leave to the world at large; private legacies are the permanent things that we leave to our friends, families, and loved ones. Sometimes there are massive contradictions in legacy. Typically, the world at large is far more interested in the nature of achievement than in the content of character. As time passes, issues of character fade. The genius British writer Charles Dickens, who wrote *A Christmas Carol, Oliver Twist,* and *A Tale of Two Cities,* was an inveterate wife-beater. Ezra Pound, the brilliant American poet, and Edgar Degas, the seminal French impressionist painter, were both raging anti-Semites. Most of us, for better or for worse, couldn't care less. We still tear up at Dickens' story every Christmas, at the melodious sounds of Pound's poems, or in the presence of the sheer beauty of a Degas landscape. For the vast majority of us, personal beliefs and conduct have little to do with a person's public legacy. Obviously, there are cases where this is not true, and a person is so sullied by their personal conduct and personal attitudes that even saintly behavior and near-miraculous achievement can be overlooked or denigrated. It doesn't happen much, though, especially in America. We are a nation that gives second chances and even third chances to those who admit unbecoming conduct and seem to make a real effort to change. We are particularly forgiving when the achievements of the person's life are transformative. For the vast majority of people, the fact that Thomas Jefferson fathered a child with one of his slaves simply pales in comparison to his achievements as a Founding Father of the nation.

However, if you happen to be a person's son, daughter, wife, or husband, that person's private legacy is far more defining than the permanent mark left on society at large. How a philandering sports figure morally harmed his family counts, for those family members, more than the number of home runs hit, knockouts achieved, or tournaments won. The brilliant medical surgeon who saves lives in the operating room but neglects her family will leave a powerful public legacy, but the private legacy will be sullied.

As we live our lives in the present, the future, and the past, it is good and valuable to keep our dual legacies in mind. Buffing one legacy without the other is merely living half a life. It is a given that very few of us will be a Florence Nightingale, Mother Teresa, Sojourner Truth, Thomas Edison, or Dr. Martin Luther King. Men and women with the power to leave truly world-changing legacies are few and far between. That said, all of us have the ability and power to leave shining, if smaller, public legacies. It is the highest of compliments to describe a person as a "good Christian," "a good Muslim," "a good Mormon," or a "good Jew." Those are public legacies. It is an equally high compliment to describe a person as a model citizen, or outstanding in their chosen field, even if that field is as modest as waiting tables or mechanic work. Excellence begets excellence; there is nothing that motivates people to achievement like seeing others achieve. At the same time, the quest for excellence transfers over from the public to the personal. Though so many of us will fall short – falling short may be a human inevitability – striving in one arena can spill over to another.

In the realm of the private legacy, nothing focuses the mind as well as the imagining of our own funerals. Lugubrious as that experience can be, the visualization of how our husbands, wives, siblings, children, and grandchildren will remember us, and how they will talk about our lives, is a wonderful reality check. The important thing to do, when we undertake this kind of self-examination, is to be honest. We must not put ourselves in the best possible light. We need to think of those things by which our children are remembering us and will remember us, and then consider whether our life's focus is actually on those things. So many of us, myself included, often worry about all the wrong things.

The way to find the right things to worry about is to listen to our loved ones when they speak to us, and what they also say in their actions. People do reasonably well at communicating what is important to them. It can be a trying thing for a parent to come to understand that the principles and values important to us may not be of equal importance to our children. So long as our children's principles and values are neither criminal nor destructive, I often counsel my clients to find a way to honor them. We have years with our children to inculcate our values. There is scarcely a child alive who could not articulate the things that are important to his or her parent. But by the time the child is a young adult, our work is largely done. What is left for us to do is create public and private legacies that can give us peace.

To that end, I have a set of simple principles that work for myself and my clients to create both a public legacy that matters and a private legacy of which we can be proud:

Don't give people more than they can handle.

Whether the person is your husband, your wife, your child, your employee, or your co-worker, the worst thing in the world is to overwhelm him or her. An overwhelmed person just feels stuck, trapped, and breathless. Movement of any kind feels impossible. The overwhelmed person feels like his or her own needs and abilities have not been taken into account. No matter what the issue, don't dump on another human being. And for goodness sake, just because we think we can handle whatever it is we're giving doesn't mean that everyone else can, too. We aren't them, and they aren't us.

Everything in life has unintended consequences; one of the unplanned-for unintended consequences of the information age is that the condition of being overwhelmed has become normalized. Ask our grandparents how many television channels they had to choose from, and they would say five or six. Many of us have five or six hundred from which to choose. We've got libraries at our fingertips, texts flying our way, minute-by-minute news updates, and notifications and instant messages coming out the wazoo. The upshot of all of this – music services where we have millions of songs from which to choose, online access to tens of thousands of magazines, bloggers firing the latest at us – is that we both get used to being overwhelmed, and claim for ourselves the right to overwhelm others. Ask anyone at any time how he or she is doing, and the answer is almost always, "Gosh, I'm so busy!" We figure that if we can manage overwhelm, others can, too.

We all know when children are overstimulated. It's visible in a slew of different ways. It's the third-grader who bursts into tears in the middle of the arcade, the first-grader who refuses to go to bed even though he has been awake for twenty hours straight, or the kid who's frantically taking notes in class though the speaker is already way ahead of him or her. We see it often when an only child is presented with a newborn little brother or sister. The oldest didn't ask to be a big brother or big sister. He or she didn't vote for this change, and if they had voted, they would have been outvoted anyway. Now, their paradigm is overwhelmed. New concepts like sharing, sacrifice, consideration, and team play come into sharp relief. For many kids, this is highly upsetting – as unsettling and unfair as if any of us were told that we would have to be a co-spouse with an unwanted other to our own husband or wife.

Kids in this situation can react badly. Tantrums are not unusual. The establishment of a pattern of domineering behavior in their own life is also common. When I see people abuse power and dominate others, my immediate suspicion is that they were eldest children who were unprepared for the arrival of younger siblings. I would be the first to say that all people are dominating to a point. But when we are yet immature, and thrust into a situation of responsibility, primitive methods of control will often emerge.

What is unusual is that we don't see this behavior for what it is: a classic overwhelm. When life changes fast, and we are unprepared for the change – what I call being role-educated – we have to scramble. Some of us scramble better than others. Some of us are like deer caught in the headlights, simply because we find the situation or the words overwhelming. The psychologists call this "being flooded," and it's a pretty good name for the condition. Often, the flood feels more like being engulfed in an emotional tsunami.

We can begin to relate to the overwhelm in a safe way when we think about people thrust into roles in life for which they do not believe that they are ready. Harry S. Truman, who became President of the United States on the sudden and unexpected death of legendary Franklin D. Roosevelt, is reported to have felt like the sun, moon, and stars had just fallen on him. On a smaller scale, I've seen video of the interior of a school bus where the driver suddenly was stricken by a heart attack, and the bus barreled along with a load of six-graders who don't know how to drive. Fortunately, the bus slowed to a safe stop, but those six-graders looked completely overwhelmed. Why wouldn't they be? They weren't equipped to do what they had to do to stay alive. They were not role-educated, not even in the minimal role of moving a gearshift to neutral or applying the brakes. When their lives were in their own hands due to circumstances beyond their control, many of them simply covered their eyes. Who could blame them?

Another arena where the overwhelm becomes both profound and routine is when children are forced to grow up too fast. Psychological development and physical development do not progress on parallel paths. We have girls in elementary school reaching puberty in the body, while their minds are still on Disney Channel. Meanwhile, their male counterparts are neither sexually nor psychologically mature. In fact, they're probably smitten more by the latest version of Pokémon than they are by the girls. It makes the girls vulnerable to guys who are older than they are; the experience of being the object of sexual attraction from a guy who's a few (or, God forbid) more than few years older than they are can be overwhelming. In the throes of that overwhelm, girls may find themselves sexually active before their time. Once sexual activity is undertaken, it has all kinds of consequences. What can be the most glorious of human connections is bastardized. I'd make the same argument when it comes to drugs and alcohol. These things, when presented to young people, and indulged in by young people, can result in a harmful overwhelm.

There are so many situations in life that result in overwhelms, where we throw too much at people to fast. It happens in employment, when a new person is brought into a job and expected to perform at the level of a seasoned veteran. It happens in education, when sheltered children go away to college for the first time. With the kind of protected and parentally involved upbringing that so many families offer their children these days, college can be an overwhelm.

Overwhelm can also come in something as grave as an unexpected medical diagnosis or as mundane as a tablet freezing up on us at the wrong moment, causing us to want to hurl the machine out the window like the world's most expensive rectangular Frisbee. It's the knock on the door that we open to two people in uniform, or the call from the hospital where a loved one was in grave condition. It's the feeling that we have as we move into the process of mourning – the funeral, the eulogy, the burial, the relatives and friends who may be as shell-shocked with grief as we are. It can come in the discovery of an extramarital affair, or a child's criminality, or a brutal financial reversal. It can come with a firing from a job, or even a non-hiring at a job for which we've prayed.

When we're overwhelmed, we react in different ways, few of them good. Some of us freeze. Some of us spring into action, but in five different directions at once. Others of us will fall back on unprepared courses of actions, often based on what we've seen from others or from our parents. However we respond, we tend to be as effective at following these courses of actions as someone who has never cooked before being asked to prepare a gourmet meal for fifty people…in two hours. Even if we know what to do, we are thoroughly unprepared to act. Then we have to deal with the fallout of our poor reactions. We may isolate and avoid relationships. We may be overly self-critical. We may be hyper-vigilant against the same thing happening again. There are as many reactions as there are people, and few of the reactions are positive.

In the face of so much trouble with overwhelms, there are three overarching lessons. First, be aware that overwhelms are inevitable. Second, try to minimize the damage of your reaction to an overwhelming situation. Some of the damage can be minimized by preparation; some of it can be minimized by enlisting the help of others, and some can be minimized by slowing down as much as possible when the situation is not life or death. Lastly, do your best not to overwhelm others, particularly your loved ones. Understand that difficult conversations are difficult enough without a surplus of emotion added into them. Know that people can't effectively talk for hours on end, and that brief can be better. Believe that as you can be flooded, so can those around you. In a world where so much is overwhelming, less is often more.

Be willing to experience anything and everything.

What is resisted will persist. So the best thing to do is to go with the experience, both so you can learn how to live with it, and so there is an opportunity for both you and the experience to change.

The best example I can offer here is the experience of grief. True grief is soul-crushing and faith-testing. It is physical, moral, intellectual and spiritual. One may be bereft to the point of tears, saddened to the point of catatonia, upset to the point where it's impossible to think, and crushed to where a concept of God seems well-nigh laughable. It's okay. Go with it. Tolerate today's feelings in the knowledge that they may not be tomorrow's feelings.

During the lead-up to the second Gulf War, then-Secretary of Defense Donald Rumsfeld was responding to reporters' questions about the absence of weapons of mass destruction in Iraq. Regardless of your feelings on that conflict, or on Mr. Rumsfeld himself, his words were instructive, prophetic, and portable to anyone's daily life. Rumsfeld was excoriated for these remarks – they actually earned him some mock awards for the least articulate use of the English language. But if one sets aside the political context, you will see that Rumsfeld makes perfect sense.

"There are known knowns; there are things we know that we know. There are known unknowns; that is to say, there are things that we now know we don't know. But there are also unknown unknowns – there are things we do not know we don't know."

How true it is! There are millions of things that we know, like how to drive a car. There are things we don't know, and know we don't know, like the step-by-step process for that car's manufacture. Then there are things that we don't know that we don't know, like that another car is going to come out of its driveway like a bat out of hell and smack into us as we're heading to work tomorrow morning.

We can make our plans for what we think we know, and life throws us curveballs. Our ability to handle the unknowns, the things that come out of left field, the things that will jolt us into a new identity, is the difference between a life lived proactively and a life lived in reaction. Our ability to take the best of our experiences and apply what we've learned to what's new can be the difference between war and peace, violence and non-violence, or family harmony and family distress.

One of the most admired men in the world was the late Nelson Mandela, the brilliant and courageous black South African leader who helped transform that country from a reviled apartheid state to a country where blacks and whites are equal in all ways. The transformation has not always been simple, and South Africa has a long way to go, but Mandela is seen universally as one of the world's truly good and transformational figures. The most striking thing about the transition is that it was accomplished more or less peacefully. It is not that South Africa swept its history under a rug. But Mandela managed to set up the country's Truth and Reconciliation Commissions so that they would seek to shed more light than heat on the nation's racially divided past.

Mandela did not come to his position easily. In fact, he was imprisoned by the apartheid regime for eighteen years at the infamous Robben Island prison because of his revolutionary activities. He was permitted one letter and one visit every six months, and spent his days literally breaking rocks into gravel. It was an upgrade when he was sent to a limestone quarry. He was not permitted to attend his mother's funeral, nor the funeral of his oldest son, who died in a car crash. Many would have been either broken or incensed by a two-decade experience like that, and come out of prison ready to retreat to a safe space or to wreak havoc on those who wrecked their lives. Yet Mandela found a way to take those prison years, extract principles of reconciliation and justice from them, and use them when he ascended to a leadership role in a new democratic South Africa. He did not resist the experience of his imprisonment; he gave it meaning and made that meaning count in his own life. In his death, he is a shining example of how to live.

So often, resistance is futile. If we tell ourselves something like, "That was the worst experience of my life; I'm never going to experience *that* again," we are setting ourselves up for a repeat. Life brings us so much that is unexpected. While there is much that is under our control, there is much more that is not. Just as a mother of a newborn cannot resist the cries and needs of the infant, we cannot resist much of what comes out way. All we can do is learn from the experience, so that if something similar happens, we are better equipped to handle it.

In my practice, I like to talk about a phenomenon I have come to call the "Judas Experience." That is, the experience of being betrayed by someone whom we have trusted. A lot of times, people will talk about having been fooled by a person. What they are really talking about is that they put trust in the person at time A, and time B, and time C, and the person came through. Then, when they trusted the person again, they found that the trust was misplaced. It is not all that far off from the experience of Jesus being betrayed by Judas.

At some point, though, life will lie to us. We will be devastated, blown away, hurt, or be betrayed by someone we trusted. If it is not a person, then it is an institution, or even a belief system. I think, on some level, we actually know that this will happen but don't want to believe it, the way that people in Southern California live as if they will not eventually experience a devastating earthquake. With luck, the quake won't happen in their lifetimes, but if it doesn't happen in their lifetimes, it will happen in the life time of their progeny, and who would actually wish for that?

I think of a client who had a terrible Judas experience in love. Her name was Nila, and she's now in her forties. She grew up in the aforementioned Southern California, near San Diego, in a good family. She was a good girl who'd done everything right, including earning a master's degree in social work. She married her longtime boyfriend after she finished graduate school. The marriage went on for years, though it took quite a while for her to get pregnant. That pregnancy happened, as it so often does, as they were in the process of adopting an infant.

The husband took the onset of the wife's pregnancy as a sign to confess to Nila that he'd been cheating on her during their entire marriage. Not just a little cheating, either – a lot of cheating. Among his sex partners were eight – that is not a typo – women Nila knew. The first instance had been during his bachelor party, in the stall of a bar bathroom on Balboa Island, with some woman he'd met at the bar. The latest had been just weeks before, in their own community.

Nila came to me in the aftermath of this disclosure. I had suspicions about the impetus for the husband's behavior, but this was not the time to talk about sex addiction. She was gutted. Her insides were torn out. She could barely breathe. She was ready to throw herself in the toilet, or put her life into reverse and get out of the mess. Of course, all these things were impossible, because she was on the verge of giving birth to this man's baby. Talk about a Judas moment. I confirmed for Nila what a horrendous situation she was now part of. It was obvious to me: Her husband had dumped the truth on her at a time of her greatest vulnerability, when she was not going to leave him. He had one more selfish goal to achieve with her: the baby.

She didn't leave. Her life, though, was seasick. She had a terrible end of her pregnancy and a non-routine C-section. She had to experience the joy of new motherhood tempered with life with a betrayer whom she thought was vile. All the time, she looked backward and asked herself if, in some way, she had contributed to the situation, or had made herself willfully blind. Her answer in both cases was negative, and I believed her. This was not one of those situations where the phone would ring with strange women on the line in the middle of the night, or where Nila caught her husband in some lie that would lead to contrition and swearing not to repeat bad behavior. Nope. That would have been too simple, and too predictable.

Nila didn't leave. She had two children to care for – one her own, and the other on the way via adoption. Ending the marriage would mean ending the adoption, and they were too far along to do that to a baby. Nila had been through so much. Much as she was infuriated with her husband, she did not want him to deprive her of a little baby who would call her "Mommy," too.

Here is how the story ended: They stayed together under the same roof for a few years. Then, Nila separated from her husband. Divorce followed. Believe it or not, they share custody. And out of respect for the children's relationship with their father, she has sworn to herself never to talk to them about their dad's behavior from the time that they were together.

Like I said, a Judas moment.

When a person has betrayed, or a person feels betrayed, it is particularly hard to use the experience for learning in a way that will make the future better. I think of my client Elena, who is in the midst of one the longest, most drawn-out divorces in the history of western jurisprudence. Elena is a fairly public figure. She's a well-known radio personality with a devoted and loyal listenership that feels like it knows her. Her husband was caught with pornography. It led to the irremediable breakdown of their marriage. I am not judging here whether the discovery of porn is a sufficient reason for a divorce, because every couple is different. Let us just say that in this case, Elena filed. She felt betrayed. Meanwhile, her to-be-ex-husband felt similarly betrayed, because he did not want to get divorced at all. He has turned into a one-man wrecking crew whose mission in life is to ruin Elena's life. It is amazing how much trouble one person can make for another if that person makes trouble-causing a priority. He files legal motions every chance he gets. The ex refuses to come to terms with the past and use the experience to move forward. He has turned himself into a suppressor. Elena's only hope is to try to manage the situation, because going on the offense herself is exactly what the ex wants. He is spoiling for a knock-down, drag-out fight, and would like it to be as public as possible. If it leads to mutually assured destruction, he doesn't care, because he already feels destroyed. There is a route for him to a better future, if he would only take what he has experienced and use it for good. Someone could show him that way. The problem is, what most would want for him is not what he wants for himself.

Which leads us to…

Don't want for others what they don't want for themselves.

If I want my alcoholic friend to stop drinking, but my friend doesn't want to give up the booze, how should I expect that to go? If I want my child to stay in school and become a nurse, and the child wants to play rock 'n' roll, how should I expect that to go? If I want my spouse to want sex seven nights a week, and my spouse is interested in two times a month, how should I expect that to go? When one's hopes and wishes for another person collide with the reality of that other person…the reality of that other person is going to win every single time.

One of the upsides of being a grownup is the desire and ability to influence others in the way that they should go. We see this most of all with our children, where the combination of our greater life experience and our children's natural desire to please us gives us a great deal of influence. Each of us may have different things that we believe are important. For some of us, it is a connection with God. For others, it's connection to our families, communities, and planet. For others it is service, artistic expression, financial achievement, or any one of myriad other things. For several golden years, what we want for children can even be achieved via raw power, at least on occasion. Who among us has not simply said, to a recalcitrant child who does not want to do X, Y, or Z, simply, "Get in the car!"

At some point, though, our desires collide with the desires of the person for whom we have a vision. Regardless of the righteousness of our vision, and no matter how well we see the water in which that person is swimming or how clearly we see their future for them in a way that they cannot see it for themselves, we should not get attached to the outcome we want. This is hard to do. All of us, particularly women, have ideas and plans for others about how they can improve their lives. It's our lot in life, and we tend to be good at it. Plus, we get attached to people, and to their outcomes. Most of all, we do not want to see our loved ones suffering, particularly when we know *the answer* and even the way to make *the answer* happen. It is painful to watch unnecessary struggling, but it is even more painful to want someone to have something that they do not want for themselves.

I know a young man, the son of a client, who was born to play football. By the time he was a junior in college, he was six foot, six inches, and 280 pounds, and could run the forty-yard dash in 4.8 seconds, which is not all that far from NFL speed. He was a feared defensive lineman who leveled running backs and quarterbacks. My client's mail was filled with recruiting letters from every major football college school in the country: UCLA, Nebraska, Miami, Florida State, Ohio State…they all wanted this boy to go to their school, and scholarships were there for the picking. My client was thrilled. Money was tight, and the idea that her son could get a full college ride, and maybe even have a lucrative career in the NFL, was a lifesaver to her.

Then her son came home one day to say he was quitting the football team. His parents were appalled. My client asked him why, and expected him to say anything other than what he did say: "Mom? I can't hit guys for no reason anymore."

My client's reaction was to wonder why he couldn't get these same feelings after he'd played his last game as a senior for Florida State University. But the fact was, her son had come to understand that he was not playing football for himself, but for others. When his parents asked him what he would want to do for himself, he surprised them again. Their hope was, if he was not to make the NFL, that he would at least go to business school. Alas, that was not their son's dream. He wanted to become a gunsmith.

That's just what he did. He has a career where he works in the design and construction of pistol and rifle silencers, he is furthering his education as a ballistic expert, and he's a happy young man. His parents are happy too…now that they've gotten over the experience of wanting something for their son that he did not want for himself.

It happens all the time. We *know* our children are meant to be lawyers, and they become writers. We *know* that they're destined for a career as a model, singer, or dancer, and they rebel against the pageants, the recitals, and the photo shoots. We believe our husbands should be more ambitious, or our wives sexier – not because of what it means to us, but what it would do for our partners. However, we cannot want these things for them more than they want them for themselves. We need to live with the sadness of our own limitations, with the reality of the other person as a whole person, and with the limited disappointment that we will feel in the other person, while at the same time loving and appreciating all of the other things that make them who they are. We can take solace in the fact that we would not presume to have others make decisions about our lives for us. We owe it to others not to be equally presumptuous.

Critical people carry secrets.

During the course of our lives, we're all going to be the subject of criticism. Criticism can be a good thing. Critical people, though, are toxic. Sometimes we can minimize our contact with them, but at other times, they invade our lives and never withdraw. It can be helpful to remember that critical people tend to operate on the principle that the best defense is a good offense. They're full of secrets themselves, and intensely fearful of what will happen when those secrets come out. If we are in a stage of life where we seem extra critical, we may need to think about our own secrets. There is not much one can do about changing how a critical person operates. As we saw in the last section, we cannot want them to become less critical than they want to be.

This phenomenon of deflecting criticism of ourselves by criticizing others is a feature of almost all political campaigns. It is one of the reasons that politics are often so off-putting. The lifeblood of the politician and the office-holder is to make decisions. Often their decisions are good ones, but sometimes they're not. At the same time, those challenging for election have histories of their own, in their families, businesses, and lives. Rather than absorb any criticism or even have to respond to it, politicians feel more comfortable going on the attack. For example, in the days and weeks after the Affordable Care Act was implemented, and people came to see that the ACA website had been so poorly designed that it was impossible for many to even examine their health care options, the Obama administration responded not with an immediate taking of responsibility, but with criticism of others. The website designers had fouled up. The website was overwhelmed. The states that had failed to set up health care exchanges were exacerbating the problem. It took weeks before the administration owned the failure.

This kind of deflection-by-criticism is not limited to one side of the aisle. Republicans are as apt to do it as Democrats. The main point is that vulnerable people will criticize in an attempt to deflect attention, and are often critical in the same areas where they maintain the most secrets. When your husband or wife is hypercritical of you about your child-rearing skills, or your management of money, or the way that you relate to your parents, or any other thing, it's safe to assume that your partner has some real vulnerabilities in the same area, and is criticizing to deflect the possibility of your seeing those vulnerabilities. If you feel like you are in a situation where you just can't win, you may have a partner who is hiding an essential truth. If you apologize profusely and get no lasting gratitude but instead more complaints, your partner may again be hiding an essential truth. You may well be part, unwittingly, of an adult game of keep-away, where the goal is to keep you away from what your partner fears could trigger a relationship crisis. Far better to admit that we aren't perfect and to accept imperfections and vulnerabilities as the price of being human. Observe what is really happening and get to the bottom of it. The truth will set you both free.

You don't get worthy ends by unworthy means.

There's nothing like a taint to ruin an achievement. We see this all the time in the world of sports, where athletes have broken world records and racked up Hall of Fame records, only to be humiliated and scorned when it comes out that steroids were involved. Lying, cheating, and stealing one's way to the top may put a person at the top in some ways, but leaves them face-down in the dumpster in others. The best in us wants to be authentic, clear, and clean. It is shocking the number of people who will express heart-rending, if private, contrition for their own personal misdeeds. They want to be authentic and clear. They want to be spiritual people. They want to look back at their public and private legacies and have them unsullied.

It is impossible to go back and undo the past – what's done is done. But it is entirely possible for all of us to live our present and our future with integrity, and even reverse many of the missteps of the past. I think of the financier Michael Milken, who did prison time and paid astronomical fines for various securities machinations. Coming out of prison, he set up a foundation with what remained of his money, started a now-respected community high school, and now is one of the most respected philanthropists in the country. What he did is what he did. But what he's doing is also what he's doing. I admire that.

It is sobering to live a stained life. The stain does not even need to be public for it to be present, though humiliation takes on a different complexion when it is public. The most public versions of those who have ascended to worthy ends by unworthy means are found in the world of sports. An entire generation of baseball players has been tainted by steroids and performance-enhancing drugs. Hitting home runs is worthy. Victories are worthy. But when those victories are achieved by bending or breaking the rules – using unworthy means – the achievements and the achievers are stained. In a different arena, the cyclist Lance Armstrong ascended to the pinnacle of his sport, conquering obstacles like cancer to get there. When he was forced to forfeit his victories and return his trophies, a whole country felt duped. That the rules against doping might have been honored more in the breach than in the observance made little difference. Sports fans everywhere felt ashamed. Lest anyone think that it is only men who'll seek victory by unworthy ends, the 1980s Olympic runner Florence Griffith Joyner faced a drug scandal of her own. Her protestations that "I never doped" fell on deaf ears, though she never failed a drug test.

People say that life is not the destination, it's the journey, and to some extent, that's right. You don't want to end up lost, but you also don't want to get to your goal by running people off the road. We all know about happy second marriages between partners who had unhappy first marriages. Sometimes those partners even meet each other when they are married to other people. It's lovely to see people find contentment, for sure. But when that contentment comes at the price of callous emotional wreckage for other people, it is hard to see that contentment as pure. It is stained.

Another thing about stains: They can fade, yes, but they never go away completely. The best way to avoid a lifelong stain is not to get dirty in the first place.

*

Five rules for living, to get to legacies we can be proud of when we're gone. From ashes to ashes and dust to dust we go, but our time on this planet can burn as brightly and as fervently as the most glorious star in the Heavens. Life can be beautiful.